There dwells an imam in every soul!
Ibadi saying

Tents and Pyramids

To Mary

Tents and Pyramids

Games and Ideology in Arab Culture
from Backgammon to Autocratic Rule

Fuad I. Khuri

Saqi Books

British Library Cataloguing in Publication Data
Khuri, Fuad I. (Fuad Ishaq)
    Tents and pyramids: games and ideology in arab culture
    from backgammon to autocratic rule.
    1. Arab countries. Politics
    I. Title
    320.9174927

    ISBN 0-86356-334-1

First published 1990 by
Saqi Books, 26 Westbourne Grove,
London W2 5RH
in association with
University Publishing House, Beirut
© Fuad I. Khuri 1990

Typeset by AKM Associates (UK) Ltd, Southall, London
Printed in Great Britain by
Billing & Sons Ltd, Worcester

Contents

Figures and Tables

A Note on Arabic Words

Proper names of people and places sometimes spelled in English with *e* or *o* will be written with *a*, *i* or *u*, following their pronounciation in classical Arabic. Thus, Mohammed will be written Muhammad. Exceptions to this rule are those words that have acquired a standardized spelling in English such as emir or emirate.

The 'ayn (') and the hamza (') are not transliterated when they occur at the beginning or end of a word. Words are italicized to indicate their foreign origin. Exact transliterations of technical words and concepts are listed alphabetically in the Glossary at the end of the book, following the system published in the *International Journal of Middle East Studies*, vol. 2, no. 4 (1971).

Plurals are written by adding an *s* to the Arabic singular form, e.g. *khanat, khanats*. Exempted from this rule are the cases in which the plural form in Arabic is more commonly used than the singular, such as *shabab* instead of *shabs* or *ahfad* instead of *hafids*.

The author is responsible for the translation of all Arabic texts. However, the Qur'anic verses have been checked with Abdullah Yusuf Ali's translation of the Qur'an published by Dar al-Arabiya, Beirut.

Preface

Tents and Pyramids is about the way the Arabs see and deal with reality, however that is defined. It argues that reality is perceived as a series of non-pyramidal structures, a matrix composed of discrete units inherently equal in value. The mental design is much like a bedouin encampment composed of tents scattered haphazardly on a flat desert surface with no visible hierarchy. (The bedouin tent is shaped like a cube or prism and does not resemble a pyramid.) Tents and pyramids are, metaphorically, opposed mental images; the first signifies the absence of hierarchy and graded authority, the second the presence of both.

In these non-pyramidal structures, authority is not built into a hierarchical arrangement where roles are subordinated to one another in a graded system; it is, rather, derived from the use of sheer physical power, with one person dominating the others. In these arrangements, strategy, manoeuvrability and tactics take precedence over office and structure. The strategy is to act in groups; the isolated are vulnerable.

Four principles of action and organization are implied here: (1) a non-pyramidal image of reality; (2) the vulnerability of isolation; (3) seeking protection in groups; and (4) tactics as more important for action than the status of office. These principles are ideological constants, 'mental structures', held to be true *sui generis*, and therefore needing no validation.

As mental structures, these principles are transferred from one sphere of action to another, from backgammon to autocratic rule.

They are expressed not only in backgammon, but also in sports and card games, in architecture and design, in poetry and prose, in charting genealogies and in laws of inheritance (Chapter 1). They can also be detected in processes of daily interaction between people, when the world is treated as if it is made up of 'family' connections (Chapter 2); in seeking marriage partners, where cousins are preferred (Chapter 3); in bargaining, where buyers and sellers confront each other with opposing interests (Chapter 4); in seeking leadership among kinsmen through the manipulation of family associations (Chapter 5); in approaching emirs and dealing with *ulama* (Chapter 6); and in maintaining power through endogamous formulations and chains of alliances (Chapter 7).

Seeing reality as a series of discrete units reflects on the authority-power structure. While playing backgammon, joining a congregation for worship, sitting in the council of emirs, buying tickets for the cinema, driving in Beirut, walking in Cairo, eating in Yemen, playing with 'worry' beads, even while thinking of the Day of Judgement—referred to in the Qur'an as 'the Day of Crowding' (*yawm al-hashr*)—I see myself as moving from one situation to another within one basic design: a rimless wheel composed of a series of dyads revolving around an axis—the dominating autocrat, the first among equals.

Where there is no hierarchy of office, no 'kings' or 'castles', people dominate one another through the strategic manipulation of custom. The tone of voice, the hands and the legs, the eyes, the seating order are all manipulated to assert your position as dominant or dominated. In Arab society you either dominate or are dominated. This applies to a wide range of daily interactions. Consider, for example, a transient episode such as taking a taxi.

When you take a taxi in London, you know exactly where to sit. It is a hierarchical situation; the client's position is in the back seat. In Arab society it is an ambivalent situation: do you take the front seat beside the driver and treat him as an equal, or do you take the back seat and treat him as an inferior? If the latter, you may not get where you wanted to go, or it is always a long way round. But if the former, the driver may feel he can 'extend his hand to your pocket'. The way out of this dilemma is to treat him as a 'brother', an equal, but simultaneously seek to dominate him, to be the 'first'.

What matters is to be 'first' among equals: figuratively, a *taiyar* (free stone) in backgammon, an 'ego' in interaction, an 'imam' in worship and an 'emir' in the courts; to be the first to buy the tickets, the first to turn off at a junction, the first to reach for food, the first to finish eating and the first to be 'judged' before God. The first to believe in Islam were assured of divine salvation. No wonder the Arabs form crowds and do not queue. Being 'first' among equals means you have built a group, a *khanat*, around yourself, and therefore will never be left alone, vulnerable to capture. Only the isolated are capturable and can be held hostage.

There are striking parallels between these mental principles and the behavioural patterns in Arab society. People of all shades and colours are praised or condemned on the basis of the tactics, manoeuvres and strategies they use. Reference is rarely, if ever, made to the use of the powers allocated to the office they occupy. Many a successful person is praised as *harbu* (tactician), one who 'knows from where to bite the shoulder'. The person comes before the office. Indeed, the person is the office. Consequently, assassination becomes an effective political instrument.

Hierarchy in Arab culture is summarized by a single imam or emir with a set of followers, each linked to him dyadically in the form of a rimless wheel (Chapter 6). As soon as the imam or emir disappears, his following disperses. The structure created by his presence swiftly collapses in his absence. With great insight, the famous fourteenth-century scholar Ibn Khaldun saw charisma as a forceful presence, describing the charismatic leader as 'the possessor of presence' (*dhu hadra*).

The lack of hierarchy forces the interactor to seek co-ordination and harmony of relationships in group membership. Isolation thus becomes vulnerability. It is a 'peril and refuge' syndrome built into the structural image of society as composed of discrete, inherently equal atoms. In other words, Arabs feel best when they are part of a group, a stone in a *khanat*. To be isolatd is to be 'cut off' or 'caught'. Many Arabs refrain from doing what they would like to do if they know they will be seen in isolation; this includes a large number of behaviours such as going to a restaurant, or to a lounge for a coffee break; or even making a trip, going for a walk or living in a particular neighbourhood.

Being alone is so feared that ostracism, excommunication and banishment are thought to be the severest forms of punishment a group can inflict upon its members. The banished person in tribal Arabia is called *su'luq* (small) in his own tribe and *muwali* (affiliated) among others—both words are derogatory. Among the Druzes of Lebanon, a breach in the religious code is punished by *azl* (isolation), and among the Ibadis of Oman and Algeria by *tabriya* (becoming innocent), which requires isolation from the group until the culprit repents.

In Arab culture, the individual seems to be caught between 'the fear of being alone', on the one hand, and the drive to be 'first among equals', an imam or emir, on the other. Because of this dilemma, people seek either to dominate or be dominated. To be first among equals is for the first to dominate the equals—the manipulation of equality (Chapter 5).

So central is the concept of dominance that a large number of the ninety-nine attributes of God signify dominance of a kind. He is the Victorious, the Conqueror, the Oppressor, the Most Glorious. Even the Merciful and the Compassionate can be taken as extensions of dominance. 'Mercy' is requested of the strong who can deliver it, not of the weak.

'Tents' and not 'pyramids' are the ingredients used by the Arab mind to organize social and physical reality. There are no pyramids and therefore no standardized rules of succession to high office. Government belongs to the powerful, the conquerors. And power rests in the control of solidarities, endogamous groups, which militates against the rise of a 'public' that holds the ruler accountable for his actions. There is no public and therefore no republic. 'President', 'king', 'sultan', 'imam', 'emir', or whatever, the governor always rules autocratically.

Reading, June 1990

1
Games and Ideology

The four principles of action and organization mentioned earlier constitute a mentally generalized phenomenon, a comprehensive system of ideology, that expresses itself in a wide variety of games, actions, interactions and cultural patterns. This chapter will try to show how these mental principles are followed in playing backgammon and other games, and how they can be generalized to other cultural patterns.

The connection between games and ideology is nowhere better expressed than in the Arab belief that backgammon is styled after the cosmos. The board, when open, is a perfect square signifying the globe; the red and black striped *khanats* (entries) signify day and night; the four houses signify the four directions or seasons; the twelve entries on one side signify the twelve months of the year; the six *khanats* in the house, the six working days of the week; the thirty stones or chips, the thirty days of the month; and the twenty-four entries, the twenty-four hours of the day (Fig. 1, App. A). The game represents the universe in all its dynamism, movement and flux. The game is moved by dice (the will of God) and from there on it is played according to rules and regulations that reflect the main themes of organization in Arab culture.

Backgammon is played in three versions: *mahbusa* (captivity)

17

which is considered to be the most sophisticated, *franjiya* (the Western) which is thought to depend more on luck than skill, and *maghrabiya* (from the Maghrib, Arab North Africa) which is simple enough to be played by children. (The rules of the game are detailed in App. A.) Implicit in any one of these versions are the four principles of action and organization, namely, the non-pyramidal image of reality, the vulnerability of isolation, seeking protection in groups, and giving precedence to tactics over office.

In backgammon, the non-pyramidal image is expressed in having no kings or queens, castles or bishops, horses or soldiers. Backgammon is a game built upon the belief that 'There dwells an imam in every soul.'[1] Each stone has the same inherent value as another. As the game proceeds, stones acquire different values depending on the position they occupy *vis-à-vis* other stones—this constitutes strategy. A stone standing alone is vulnerable and could therefore be caught or captured. The safest position is to be part of a group (*khanat*), which can be made with a minimum of two stones. If a third stone is added to a *khanat*, it can then move freely from one position to another without endangering the safety of the other stones (the group). This is why the third stone in a *khanat* is called imam or *taiyar*, i.e. the one who flies freely, meaning as free as a bird. (In Arab lore, birds are the freest of all creatures.)

The strategy is to move the stones across the board from one player's house to the opponent's without being captured or caught, and while doing so a player may be able to capture the opponent's stones. In *mahbusa*, the captured stone remains captive until the *taiyar* moves to a new position. In *franjiya*, it has to go back to its base before moving to a new position. Isolated stones are vulnerable so long as they are not grouped in *khanats*.

Appendices B and C discuss two more games, *dama* (or draughts: Fig. 2) and *man'ala* (Fig. 3), which are played with almost the same implicit principles; just the milieu is different. In these two games, the strategy is to work out formulas by which chequers in *dama* and pebbles in *man'ala* are isolated and then 'eaten'. The same themes of organization for action prevail: no structured hierarchies, inherently equivalent discrete units, no graded offices, an emphasis on strategy and manoeuvrability, seeking protection in groups, and winning by capturing or 'eating'.

Native sports and card games are played with the same mental principles. [2] Of these I shall deal briefly with only two sports, *beel* and *asir*, and a card game called *basra*. I must stress here that I am concerned only with native games, and not with the internationally commercialized games of today which, in the Arab world as elsewhere, are supplanting the local ones.

Beel is played with one implicit, cognitive formula: 'One against all' (see App. D for details). It demonstrates many principles of action and organization that pertain to the making of the person in Arab culture. Of these principles the emphasis on 'being first among equals' is the most pressing.

My aunt, Kafa Khuri, who taught for 64 years in the village school, is well remembered for the phrase she used to repeat in her speech on 1 October of every school year: 'Walk like an *aliph*, talk like an *aliph*, be an *aliph*.' *Aliph* is the first letter of the Arabic alphabet—a vertical line with a straight, upright posture. The people who normally responded favourably to the teacher's speech were the parents who all claimed their son was the first in class. (Daughters do not count; the sons are the public pride of the family.)

The emphasis on being 'first' dominates the thinking of the Arabs to such an extent that, throughout their history, they have never been able to develop a clear and lasting pyramidal, formal structure of government. Succession to power and authority has always been problematic. The emphasis on being first necessarily implies the second part of the phrase, 'among equals'. If everyone is to be 'first', the struggle must then be between 'equals', much like chequers on a *dama* board or stones in backgammon.

The outward emphasis on group achievement in Arab culture is only meant to camouflage and suppress the strong drive for individualization. In other words, 'ride the tide', with an emphasis on 'ride' or 'being on top', is closer to reality than 'sail with the wind' like everybody else. 'Unless you are a wolf, you will be eaten by wolves' is a still better prescription. The Arabs are 'never alone but always lonely'. 'We are a country of officers and no soldiers,' said the late Lebanese prime minister Sami al-Sulh.

Like many loners in the world, the Arabs surround themselves with friends, but allow none to come too close. Coming close is dangerous; it exposes the private. In other words, while 'getting along is easy, love is difficult'. Many an Arab male approaches love as if it were a one-way traffic: she loves me and that is enough. This is not to say that Arab culture is *in toto* a 'loner' culture. I am simply describing the kind of cultural environment in which Arabs are brought up. 'If partnership is blessed, two men would marry one woman,' stresses an Arab saying.

Asir (App. E) and *basra* (App. F), like other native games, are symbolically no different from *beel*. They are built on the same mental principle: the individualization of achievement in non-hierarchical structures. Much like *beel*, *asir* has no 'centre', 'wing', 'back' or 'goalkeeper'; there is no graded structure with variegated authorities or responsibilities allocated to individual players. Except for the initial division of teams into 'us' and 'them', and the subsequent territorial divisions, all players are 'equal'. This is to say that the same performance is expected of every one of them. The difference between one player and another lies in the relative skill of performance, not in the complex architecture of the game.

The games played in childhood, between the ages of 6 and 12, require physical strength and speed; those played in adulthood, from 13 onwards, are played on chairs around tables. (In Arabic, the category 'youth' (*shabab*) includes everybody between 6 and 60.) However, the same mental formula—individualization of achievement in non-pyramidal structures—is continuously implied in all games. Adult native games include backgammon, *dama*, *man'ala* and a variety of card games. A teenager who wants to assert his manhood often chooses to play these games with adults.

Playing together, or better against each other, neutralizes and equalizes the status of the players and momentarily suspends the formality of interaction between them. Personally, I only started to feel at ease with my father-in-law when we began playing backgammon together. Swear-words, which equalize the status between interactors, are much more permissible over a game of backgammon than in ordinary forms of interaction.

The absence of formal hierarchical structures in games—the absence of 'centres' and 'wings', 'kings' and 'castles'—reflects a generalized image of reality that extends to various cultural patterns. As previously mentioned, the Arab mind seems to see reality as composed of discrete, atomized units inherently identical in value: an imam in every soul.

Designs and patterns are thus created by arranging the same unit or motif in different shapes. Arab monolithic architecture is built with the aid of a single motif, the arch, writ large in different directions. Cordova in Andalusia, the Qurawiyeen Seminary at Fez and al-Azhar Mosque in Cairo are all living examples of Arab architectural designs.

The Arabs see reality as composed of 'tents' and not 'pyramids'. Consequently, human society is conceived of as an *umma* (community) made up of 'brothers' following an imam rather than a state or states with a graded authority system. The word *umma* is derived from the verbal root *amma*, meaning to follow or to come to, which implies a dyadic relationship between an individual and a leader. There are no pyramids and therefore no primogeniture. Every child is entitled to inheritance as a birthright, with one difference between the sexes: the share of one male is equivalent to that of two females.

This atomized image of reality is also expressed in classical writing where punctuation, which indicates subordination and superordination and separates dependent from independent clauses, is entirely absent. The Qur'an was originally written without commas, full stops or exclamation marks. Meanings flow on without interruption of thought. Every verse stands alone as a complete unit of revelation and is dealt with as such by Qur'anic interpreters.

Likewise, in poetry and prose and other forms of literature, verses and ideas stand uniquely alone, complete bits of thought that do not link hierarchically to a centralized theme. They are beads, not cathedrals. There are no centralized themes and therefore no paragraphs. Arabs write without paragraphs; sentences and half sentences flow on and on.

In the same vein, Arab novels dramatize the experience of single heroes, and the stage is dominated by the massive presence of single actors. When the 'imam' actor disappears from the stage, the audience gets bored. Native theatres are animated by single narrators, called *hakawatis*, who alone try to depict the plot from start to finish. Arab writers have never excelled in drama, which requires co-ordination between a variety of hierarchically arranged roles. Most of the plays in Beirut's theatres before the 1975 Lebanese war were either translated from Western sources or inspired by them. No wonder the Arabs invented algebra and not calculus; they have the expertise to handle variations ordered by single, not multiple, equations.

The lack of formal hierarchical structures is also expressed in many social, cultural and religious practices. Arabs see society as a 'community' (*umma*) composed mainly of 'brothers' and 'sisters'. Rank is expressed in a series of seniority statuses captured in dyadic family relationships (Chapter 3). Indeed, the word class (*tabaqa*), which signifies social gradation, is used in the Qur'an to distinguish between the layers of the earth, the moon and the skies, and not between categories of human beings, rich and poor, elites and masses. Human beings are distinguished on the basis of religious dogma, Muslims versus non-Muslims, and Muslims are distinguished from each other on the basis of the strength of their faith.

Indeed, classes, which imply social hierarchy, are so confused that status titles which signify some kind of superordination, such as *bey*, *pasha*, *agha*, *afandi* or *za'im*, are used in two opposed senses: formally, to indicate high status, or jokingly, to indicate low status. Thus, you may call a superior *bey* or *za'im* because he is one; or you may call a subordinate, such as a waiter in a restaurant, *bey* or *za'im* because you are one (Chapter 2). It is intentionally confusing.

The vision of society as composed of brothers is reinforced by several cultural precepts that see 'the person' as a link in a chain, and the chain as a single solidarity (Chapter 7). The concept of solidarity and internal cohesion is not pictured as a pyramid; it is rather depicted as a 'seriation of individuals' arranged in various horizontal forms. Consider the following words that all signify solidarity: *silsila* (chain), *tasalsul* (descent) and *habl* (rope or cable) as revealed in the Qur'an (3/103): 'And hold fast, all of you together, to the cable [*habl*] of Allah and do not separate.'[3]

The same phenomenon can be observed in religious practice. Arab Muslims congregate for prayer as discrete individuals guided by an imam. The imam is recruited by the congregation on the spot, either as a sign of respect for his social standing or in deference to his religious knowledge. He stands 1 or 2 metres in front of the congregation to lead them in prayer. An imam is a model to imitate. The word imam can have several meanings: the first camel that leads the caravan, the rope used to set building blocks in order following the corner stone, and the big bead that links all the others at the top in a single chain.

In collective prayer, the imam is not physically segregated from the body of worshippers by standing on an elevated platform or at an altar. On the contrary, he is at the same level as the rest of the congregation. Exactly like a player in *beel* or *asir*, or like a *taiyar* stone in backgammon, he is singled out for a transient role and is not appointed to a permanent office. The congregation, in turn, follows no clear-cut seating order: custom dictates that it is 'first come first served'. The choice is the worshippers' except on formal occasions where public dignitaries take the front rows. This lack of hierarchy in seating is likewise followed in Sufi forms of worship or other religious assemblies. In these kinds of gatherings, circular forms that reaffirm the ethics of brotherhoods are definitely preferred (Chapter 6).

Given this non-pyramidal image of reality, queuing becomes a problem. Arabs do not queue; they form crowds. They crowd at traffic lights, post office windows, information booths, ticket bureaux, cinema exits, shopping centres, and to cheer leaders and face the final trial before God. The Day of Crowding (*yawm al-hashr*) is a blessed day; it is the Day of Judgement.

There remains the question: in the absence of hierarchic structures, how do people seek to become imams, firsts among equals? Metaphorically, how can they be a *taiyar* in backgammon, a '*dama*' in *dama*, a 'captain' in *beel* or *asir*, an *ashush* in *basra*, or, for that matter, an imam in prayer? These positions are achieved through, first, dominating individual solidarities, and then striking alliances with higher ranks, thus creating a constellation-like syndrome of power relations. When two Arabs meet, the question is who dominates whom?

In fact, the whole theory of social differentiation rotates

around the strong and the weak. Client tribes are weak tribes, and the strong are patrons (*usul*). The proletariat in Muslim Arab society is referred to as the 'made weak' (*mustad'afun*), not the poor. 'Poverty' is an attribute of man, and 'wealth' an attribute of God. A community is considered to be Muslim if it fulfils two conditions: first, formally to follow Islamic law, and second, to be governed by a Muslim imam, even if the majority of people who live in it are non-Muslim. The emphasis on 'power' and 'dominance' is very clear.

Likewise, the non-Muslims in an Islamic community are 'the protected' (*ahl-dhumma*) who wield no power. They are barred from power-oriented offices, irrespective of their wealth. Although religious minorities in Islamic states tend to be economically better off than Muslims (which cannot be said of minorities in non-Islamic societies), the important point is that they have no power.

The bulk of behavioural characteristics imposed upon non-Muslims in Islamic states always signify lack of power. They are forbidden from carrying arms, occupying high office in government, joining the army, marrying Muslim girls, riding horses, living in the upper section of towns and building houses higher than Muslim houses. The tax non-Muslims pay is a *jizya* (form of punishment) and not a *zakat* (form of sacrifice) for God.

These behavioural characteristics are likewise imposed by the strong upon the weak, by the dominant upon the dominated, irrespective of religious affinities. It is a comprehensive system of interaction that expresses itself in the domination of God over man, and of man over the natural world and his fellow men.

2
The World as Family

People play games not only on boards, but also in society as a part of the process of interaction. The logic either to dominate or be dominated in a 'first-among-equals' environment creates ambivalence and unease among the interactors. While trying to be first by dominating others, an interactor contradictorily tries to create an atmosphere of closeness and equality. It is a process of continuous oscillation between one position and another. Muʿawiya bin Abi Sufyan, the founder of the Umayyad dynasty, has often been praised for saying:

> Were there to be a hair between me and the people, I wouldn't let it be cut. Should they pull, I ease off; should they ease off, I pull.

In passing episodes of human interaction, equality is not a given; it is reached through a complex process of generalizing kinship terms to the whole universe around the interactor. It is a process in which people become brothers and sisters, aunts and uncles, nieces and nephews, first and second cousins—relations that affect behaviour and shape actions to the advantage of actors and interactors.[1]

The phrase 'the world as family' illustrates how kinship terms in day-to-day, person-to-person interactions are used to express equality, closeness and a wide variety of dispositions, temperaments and moods. This expression is instrumental in the sense that it is used to accomplish specific goals. Chapter 4 demonstrates how it is used to affect choice behaviours in market situations and Chapter 5 shows how it is used to build up a person's political career. The use of kinship terms is a comprehensive process of interaction built upon highly patterned sets of assumptions about the actor and the interactor—'actor' refers to the person who initiates the process, the subject of interaction, and 'interactor' to the person or persons towards whom it is directed, the object of interaction.

Kinship terms are used for many purposes: legal, behavioural, corporational, linguistic and interactional.[2] The interactional approach, which concerns us here, focuses on the meaning and usage of kinship terms in different contexts of interaction between kin and non-kin. As forms of address or reference, kinship terms are used to convey friendliness, animosity, anger, formality, seriousness, sarcasm, intimacy, politeness, disrespect, status, hierarchy, equality, closeness or distance. It is a world in itself. Terms such as *akh* (brother), *amm* (father's brother), *khal* (mother's brother) and others not only indicate actual referents in the kinship structure, but are also used by extension to reflect and generate a wide range of feelings and attitudes between interactors. For comparative purposes, the meaning and usage of status terms in person-to-person interactions will be discussed first.

Status Terms

Whereas status terms imply differentiation and distance between interactors, kinship terms imply closeness and equality of status even in those situations where seniority takes precedence. An actor who addresses or refers to another as *amm* establishes equality of social standing, but simultaneously expresses deference and seniority. If it is his superior who is referred to as *amm*, he begs equality and accordingly invites ridicule. The actor here falsely assumes either that he is as high in status as his superior or that the superior is as low in status as he is. Interactors who belong to different social strata address or refer to each other in status terms, not kinship terms. If they belong to the same social stratum, whether high or low, they use kinship terms. Using kinship terms in stratified situations of interaction is considered an insult to the high-status person and pretentious behaviour on the part of the low-status person.

Status terms may be used in three different ways: direct address, self-reciprocity or by extension. Direct address indicates the flow of codes from the low- to the high-status person, such as a commoner addressing or referring to a notable as *bey*, *pasha* or *afandi*. Self-reciprocity indicates the flow of codes in the opposite direction, i.e. from the high- to the low-status person, such as a notable addressing or referring to a commoner as *bey*, *pasha* or *afandi*. Extension occurs in those situations where interactors wish to induce either closeness and friendly relationships or, on the contrary, distance and formal attitudes.

The use of status terms in person-to-person interactions varies with their referents: formal office, social status, secular or religious meanings. Table 1 gives a detailed summary of these variations. Formal office indicates bureaucratic structures and graded authority systems; social status indicates differentiation based on the accumulation of social inequalities. Within the same title category, usages vary from case to case depending on the nuances of relationships that bind interactors together.

Secular and religious titles that imply formal office (categories II and V in Table 1) are used in direct address to express formality and distance irrespective of the contents of relationships between interactors. In stratified situations of interaction, friends and enemies, kin and non-kin, neighbours and strangers refer to holders or formal office by their titles. If used in a self-reciprocal way, these terms express disgust and dissatisfaction with the performance of inferiors and subordinates. In this sense they become acts of scolding, admonishment or castigation. A *za'im* (national leader) who is dissatisfied with the performance of a follower addresses or refers to him as *za'im*, thus expressing his disgust and discontent. By the same token, members of a university department might refer to the secretary as chairman if she interferes in administrative affairs that obviously belong to the faculty.

If used in an extension form—namely, to address or refer to people who do not occupy formal office—these terms neutralize status, nullify social differentiation and establish instead a form of equality between interactors. Used in this sense, formal office titles are exchanged only between friends. It is a gesture of friendship, and a measure of it, to address or refer to a person as *fakhama* (president), *dawla* (prime minister), *ma'ali* (minister), *fadila* (Muslim shaikh), *samaha* (imam or mufti) or *ghibta* (Christian patriarch) if the addressee or referent does not empirically occupy the appropriate office. Outside friendship ties, the use of formal office titles in extension forms is insulting—it is seen as expressing sarcasm and ridicule. Excepted from this rule is the term *ra'is*, meaning president, which may also imply formal office and social status, depending on the context. The term *ra'is* (also pronounced *rayyis*) largely acquired this current usage in Egypt under Nasser, the president who came to symbolize collective brotherhood, which is a form of equality.

Titles that imply secular social status—namely, *bey*, *pasha*, *za'im*, *shaikh* (chief), *agha* and *ra'is*—are used in an extension form to nullify social distinctions between friends and non-friends alike, even where the interactors do not empirically share the

Table 1: Classification and Meaning of Status Terms

Category[a]	Title	Verbal root	Meaning of root	Referent	FO	SS	ST	RT[b]
I	*za'im*	*za'ama*	assume	community leader		*	*	
I	*amir*	*amara*	order	tribal chief		*	*	
I	*ra'is*	*ra'isa*	head	1. president	*	*	*	
				2. chairman	*		*	
				3. principal	*		*	
I	*bey*	(Turkish origin)		notable		*	*	
I	*pasha*	(Turkish origin)		notable		*	*	
I	*afandi*	(Turkish origin)		notable		*	*	
I	*agha*	(Turkish/Persian origin)		notable		*	*	
II	*jalala*	*jalla*	rise high	king	*		*	
II	*fakhama*	*fakhuma*	become great	president	*		*	
II	*dawla*	*dala*	rotate power	prime minister	*		*	
II	*ma'ali*	*ala*	elevate	minister	*		*	
III	*shaikh*	*shakha*	become old	1. chief		*	*	
III				2. notable		*	*	
III				3. Islamic jurist	*			*
III	*sayyid*	*sada*	prevail	1. master		*	*	
				2. descendant of imam		*	*	
III	*qutb*	*qataba*	collect	1. great leader		*	*	
				2. Sufi leader	*			*
III	*khatib*	*khataba*	lecture	1. public speaker	*		*	
				2. imam	*			*
IV	*mulla*	(Persian origin)		Shi'a specialist	*			*
IV	*imam*	*amma*	come to	1. leader in prayer		*		*
				2. divine designation	*			*
				3. top Shi'a official		*		*
IV	*mufti*	*afta*	solve	Islamic jurist	*			*
IV	*mujtahid*	*ijtahada*	interpret	Shi'a jurist	*			*
V	*fadila*	*fadula*	be virtuous	religious shaikh	*			*
V	*samaha*	*samuha*	forgive	imam or mufti	*			*
V	*niyafa*	*nafa*	overlook	Christian bishop	*			*
V	*ghibta*	*ightabata*	be happy	Christian patriarch	*			*

a.
 I   Secular social status titles
 II Secular titles of formal office
 III Combination of secular & religious titles
 IV Religious social status titles
 V   Religious titles of formal office

b. FO = Formal office
 SS = Social status
 ST = Secular title
 RT = Religious title

same social standing. Whereas formal office titles are used extendedly only between friends, social status titles are used in situations of interaction involving buyers and sellers in the *suq* (Chapter 4), customers and waiters in restaurants, passengers and taxi-drivers, and between acquaintances who have not come to know each other well at conferences or other formally or informally organized short-term sessions. These situations require a minimum of mutual trust and confidence in order for the process of interaction to be successful. A seller addressing a buyer as *bey, shaikh* or *pasha*; a waiter addressing a customer, or a taxi-driver addressing a passenger, as *agha, za'im, afandi, sayyid*, or vice versa—these forms of address establish, reinforce and generate a transitory atmosphere of mutual trust and confidence that helps interactors conclude their transactions successfully.

Only secular social status titles (category I, Table 1) are subject to this pattern of usage by extension; titles with religious implications are used in their proper settings. Whether reflecting social status or formal office, *mulla, qutb, mufti, mujtahid, imam* and *khatib* are used to address or allude to their specific referents. They are used in direct address to express formality, respect and distance; and self-reciprocally to express disgust, dissatisfaction and discontent. Like formal office titles, religious titles that imply social status are used extendedly to reflect joking relationships between friends. Non-friends do not joke, at least not in this way; the use of religious social status terms between non-friends expresses sarcasm and ridicule.

Kinship Terms

The use of kinship terms establishes equality between interactors without eliminating deference, seniority, formality and sometimes distance. Their usage in this sense corresponds to the usage of social status titles in extended forms with one basic difference: whereas social status titles temporarily suspend status differentiations and establish instead an atmosphere of mutual trust and confidence, kinship terms used extendedly assert equality in status while expressing formality, seniority and deference. Not all kinship terms are subject to this pattern of usage; some categories are never used extendedly to refer to non-kin. In this connection, four categories can be discerned: terms referring to family origin; collective kinship terms denoting groups of various sizes and genealogical depths; terms derived from and based on descent relations; and terms derived from and based on affinal (marriage) and ritualistic relations.

Terms of Family Origin

Terms signifying family origin include *sulala* (genealogy), *asl* (origin), *nasab* (patrilineality), *hasab, asbat, ahfad* and *salaf* (all meaning predecessors) and *khalaf* (successors). As shown in Fig. 4, *nasab* refers to male ancestors traced through the father, *hasab* to male ancestors traced through the mother, *asbat* to male descendants traced through daughters and *ahfad* to male descendants traced through sons. In Arab culture, family origins may be traced to place names such as Sham (Damascus), Ghassan (Huran) and Yaman (Yemen), to names of tribal ancestors such as Qahtan and Adnan, or to important religious figures including the Prophet, Imam Ali or his descendants, or to any one of the Prophet's early supporters called the *sahaba* (companions) and *ansar* (partisans).

Terms of origin may characterize individuals or groups: a person or a group is said to possess or lack *asl, nasab* or *hasab*. To possess these is an expression of high standing in society and a measure of achievement; to lack them is a measure of low standing. Upon becoming rich or socially prominent, individuals and groups automatically strike historical roots and acquire long genealogies. The ethnographic record on Arab culture shows that high status and long genealogies are clearly interconnected phenomena among nomads, peasants and city-dwellers.[3] In Bahrain, for example, people divide themselves into three categories: *ansab*, *la-ansab* and *bani-khudair*. The term *ansab*, which means those who have clear genealogies and established pedigrees (*ashab asl*), refers to the ruling family and their allies of tribal origin. *La-ansab*, which refers to those who possess confused genealogies, indicates Arab families who have no direct claims to tribal origins. *Bani-khudair*, meaning 'the sons of green', refers to those who have no claim to tribal Arab origin, the low classes of Bahrain. Significantly, *akhdar*, which means green in Arabic, was used to refer to black people, often of African extraction and perhaps slave origins.

In interactional processes, the use of *asl* (origin) indicates power, competence, skill, prominence, honesty, generosity and/or commitment to principles. A person who demonstrates any one of these good qualities is said to be 'the possessor of origin' (*sahib asl*). By contrast, the person who demonstrates none of these attributes is said to be 'lacking in origin' (*bila asl*). In this sense, *asl* is believed to be the property of people, horses, dogs, camels and hawks. An *asil* person, horse, dog, camel or hawk is one whose ancestors are known over many generations; he is superior to his own kind in looks, qualities and performance.

Other terms of origin, such as *salaf*, *khalaf*, *asbat* and *ahfad*, are used as points of reference to praise or condemn individual achievements or behaviour—it is a system of personal evaluation. Just as a favourable action is welcomed with the phrase *wa ni'ma al-salaf wa al-khalaf* (How graceful the predecessors and successors), an unfavourable action is condemned by the phrase *wa bi'sa al-salaf wa al-khalaf* (How miserable the predecessors and successors). The phrase 'How graceful the predecessors' is used to praise a person's action at two referent points, the actor and his or her predecessors. The phrase 'How graceful the successors' praises the interactor and both his or her predecessors and successors.

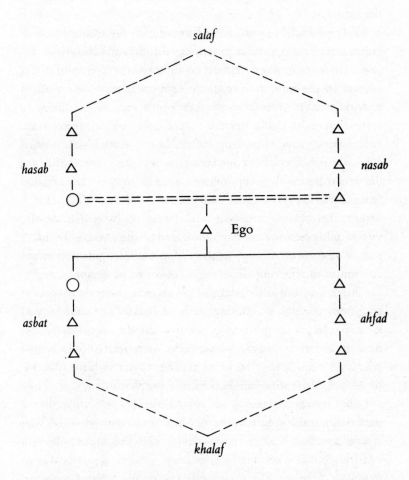

Figure 4: Terms of Family Origin

In a favourable context, *salaf* and *khalaf* mean the same thing. In a negative context, however, the two terms do not carry the same meaning. The phrase 'How miserable the predecessors' condemns the interactor and his or her ancestors, whereas the phrase 'How miserable the successors' condemns him while praising the predecessors.

Salaf and *khalaf* are often used to indicate the transmission of cultural traditions, private practices, customs and habits from one generation to another. If used to indicate the continuity of a custom in the same family, these terms acquire an element of historicity that often accompanies high status or the claim to status. To claim that a Persian carpet, a copper or bronze tray, coffee cups, ways of making coffee, lasting friendships, mutual visits, the public celebration of feasts, or serving a special dish on a particular holiday are kept or done because they are transmitted from *salaf* to *khalaf* is to claim prominence in society. Whether true or not, these claims are sociological gestures by which socially visible achievements are communicated to the outside world. A person's *asl* traced through *nasab* and/or *hasab* is augmented by the continuity of traditions from predecessors to successors.

Unlike *salaf* and *khalaf*, which may refer to the transmission of traditions through generations, *asbat* and *ahfad* are used only as kinship referents to praise or condemn individual actions. *Asbat* is used to refer to religious traditions or maternally inherited characteristics. In the first sense, it refers to the Shi'a imams born to Ali bin Abi Talib from Fatima, the Prophet's daughter. They are collectively known as *sibt al-rasul*, the Prophet's daughter's sons, who are deeply revered in Shi'a theology and ritual. *Sibt al-rasul* are believed to possess not only the highest human qualities, but also knowledge, devotion and divinity. If used in an extension form to refer to people who do not claim a religious origin, such as saying in direct address or reference that a person is from the Prophet's *sibt*, this indicates the possession of admirable human qualities. I have heard this said in praise of behaviour or an act with obvious religious connotations, such as giving *sadaqa* (alms) or making a generous donation to the building of a mosque, religious school, shrine or cemetery.

If, on the other hand, the expression *sibt al-rasul* is used to refer to maternally inherited characteristics, it often has a negative connotation, implying condemnation of unfavourable behaviour or acts. The phrase *al-sibt al-la'in* (the accursed *sibt*) is used extendedly to condemn the behaviour or an act of a person whose *asbat* linkages are unknown. In praising an actor's behaviour by referring to his or her known maternal origin, the term *hasab* (male ancestors through the mother's line) is used instead of *sibt*. In fact, one of the meanings of *hasab* is the inheritance of good qualities.[4] In other words, the tendency is to condemn behaviour or an act by referring to the person's *sibt* (the daughters' sons) and to praise it by referring to his or her *hasab* (the mothers' fathers).

The term *ahfad* has a much more restricted usage than *asbat*. In interaction, it is often used as a kinship referent to imply, much like *hasab*, the possession of good qualities. An army officer, for example, may address his soldiers as the *ahfad* of Salah al-Din (the Muslim sultan who ousted the Crusaders from Syria), meaning that they are, or he wants them to be, brave, confident and victorious.

Collective Kinship Terms

In day-to-day, person-to-person interactions, collective kinship terms are used in two ways: to establish the social identity of interactors and to generate an atmosphere of equality between them. As an identity, collective kinship terms (Table 2) indicate the position of a person on a morally graded system and socially stratified scale. Claims to *asl* (origin) are made by individuals about family groups. Although *asl, hasab* and *nasab* are used to indicate the prominent qualities of individuals and not of groups, the process of establishing origin and claiming historical roots through long genealogies refers to kinship groups and not to individuals. This is why families, clans and lineages as collective bodies are said to have 'origin', but the claim to such origin is

Table 2: Collective Kinship Terms

Term	Verbal root	Meaning of root	Kinship referent	Non-kinship referent
usra	*asara*	capture	nuclear family	--
bait	*bata*	stay	home; household; family	household
ahl	*ahala*	rehabilitate	parents; family	family of origin; country
a'ila	*ala*	provide	nuclear family; extended or stem families of all sizes; children (*iyal*)	unity of interests
jubb	*jabba*	cut; fertilize	lineage	clusterer; well
ashira	*ashara*	seduce; tease	clan	--
qabila	*qabala*	seek direction	tribe	--
qurba	*qaruba*	be close	relatives	neighbours; socially close
Tribal sections				
sha'b	*sha'aba*	drift	section of a tribe	people; nation
batn	(noun)	belly	,,	--
fakhidh	(noun)	thigh	,,	--
fasila	*fasala*	separate	,,	species
raht	*rahata*	stay	,,	--
amara	*ammara*	build	,,	building

made by prominent individuals in the family and not by ordinary kinsmen. If the latter made such claims, they would invite ridicule.

Inquiries about family affiliation are designed to place the interactors in the proper moral and social perspective. The rank of particular family groups is always known locally and sometimes nationally, depending upon the general status of the family in question. Knowledge of the ranking order of family groups facilitates interaction between locals and between them and strangers. Families of high status are gratified if they discover that outsiders know the family tree and the places individuals occupy in it. Before I went to Bahrain to carry out field research in 1974–75, I memorized the genealogy of the Al-Khalifa, the ruling family of Bahrain, which proved extremely helpful in establishing a rapport with Al-Khalifa government officials. A knowledge of names and origins constitutes the key element of interaction upon which social structure and control are built.[5]

Because of its importance in interaction, family affiliation is camouflaged if it places the person at a disadvantage. While people of lower status seek affiliation with broader tribal divisions such as *sha'b* or *qabila*, people of higher status seek affiliation with smaller divisions such as *jubb, ashira, raht* or *fasila*.[6] Outside locally known genealogies, however, these terms do not have the same referents, which adds confusion to family affiliation and therefore introduces an element of flexibility in interaction. In corporational studies on kinship, this confusion in the referents of collective terms is functionally a product of segmentary systems. Using the same term to refer to kinship groups of different sizes and genealogical depths facilitates the processes of fusion and fission, depending upon the availability of resources and the strategy of collective actions. This confusion is well illustrated in Ali's work (1976: 509–28) on tribal divisions in Arabia at the rise of Islam summarized in Fig. 5. Here, category I refers to the broadest, most all-encompassing tribal divisions and category V to the smallest; the others are segmentary groups that fall in between.

The second usage of collective kinship terms—namely, to generate an atmosphere of equality between interactors—applies to those terms that carry non-kinship referents: *ahl, a'ila, qurba* and *sha'b* (Table 2). These terms are used by extension to generate closeness, equality in status, unity of interests and internal solidarity. They are mostly used by politicians who seek consensus, or wish to marshal support, recruit followers, build favourable public images and acquire collective identities. In this

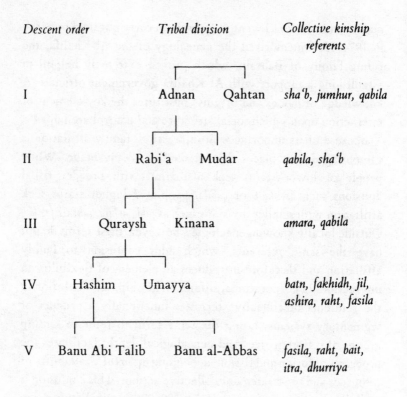

Descent order   *Tribal division*   *Collective kinship referents*

I   Adnan   Qahtan   *sha'b, jumhur, qabila*

II   Rabi'a   Mudar   *qabila, sha'b*

III   Quraysh   Kinana   *amara, qabila*

IV   Hashim   Umayya   *batn, fakhidh, jil, ashira, raht, fasila*

V   Banu Abi Talib   Banu al-Abbas   *fasila, raht, bait, itra, dhurriya*

Figure 5: Kinship Referents of Tribal Divisions

sense, the usage of these terms is uni-directional and cannot be reversed. Politicians address or refer to their supporters and followers as if they together formed one family (*a'ila*) and one people (*sha'b*), one group of parents (*ahl*) and relatives (*qurba*). Their followers, however, do not reciprocate these forms of address or reference. To do so would be offensive, an act of trespass over rights and privileges, and would therefore invite ridicule. In other words, when a leader seeks closeness in an effort to expand his constituency, his supporters reciprocate by seeking distance. Obviously, for a supporter to reciprocate with terms implying closeness would be to compete, not to show support.

Descent, Affinal and Ritualistic Terms

Descent terms refer to blood relations generated by birth, and affinal terms to in-law relations generated by marriage. Ritualistic terms are formed through religiously sanctioned ceremonies. Descent terms (Fig. 6) are used in direct address to refer to the exact kinship relation in question, such as a son addressing or referring to his father as *ab*, his grandfather as *jadd*, his maternal uncle as *khal*, his maternal aunt as *khala*, and so on. These are proper usages that signify the behavioural expectations in that particular process of interaction. In their self-reciprocal form—such as a father addressing or referring to his son or daughter as *ab*, a mother calling her son or daughter *umm*, or a paternal uncle or aunt calling a niece or nephew *khal* or *khala*— they indicate the height of love, affection and intimacy. Such usages occur between different filial generations and not between collaterals or siblings.

Descent terms, however, permeate a wide variety of interactions between non-kin, sometimes cutting vertically across social classes and different statuses. The general rule of usage in their extended form is governed by the very relationships that characterize interaction between kin (see Chapter 3). In other words, an actor who addresses or refers to an interactor as *amm* or *ukht* generates behavioural expectations that characterize uncle-nephew or brother-sister relationships. These extensions are made within the same age, sex and status categories that govern kinship referents. In other words, an interactor is addressed or referred to as *amm* or *ukht* if he or she is of the same age, sex and status as the actor's uncle or sister. Equivalence in status is necessary because the usage of kinship terms, as mentioned earlier, reflects and creates an atmosphere of equality between interactors.

Filial generation

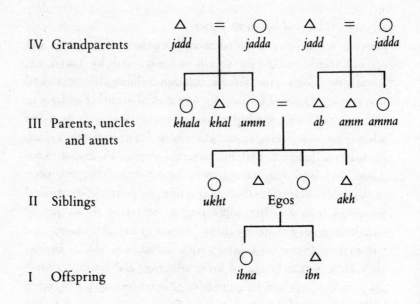

Figure 6: Descent Terms

The behavioural content of descent relationships is difficult to describe in precise terms; it varies with the situation, income group, locality, status group, childrearing practices, personal moods and temperaments (see Chapter 3). What follows is a discussion of the broad, normative aspects of behavioural expectations. The use of descent terms in extension forms falls into five different categories—the extension of relationships between: (1) siblings; (2) parents and children; (3) actor and paternal uncle or aunt; (4) actor and maternal uncle or aunt; and (5) actor and paternal grandfather or grandmother, or maternal grandfather or grandmother.

The use of the sibling terms *akh* (brother) and *ukht* (sister) between non-kin interactors reflects and generates reserve and distance, but simultaneously establishes an atmosphere of equality and trust. It is a measure of politeness and respect to address or refer to an interactor as *akh* or *ukht* if he or she is the same age and status as the actor. Reserve and distance can be somewhat softened by using the possessive case, *akhi* (my brother) or *ukhti* (my sister).[7] The plural forms *ikhwan* or *akhawat*, which are used to indicate collective solidarity and unity of interests, generate familiarity and closeness more than the singular forms, as, for example, in the Qur'an (49/10): *al-mu'minun ikhwatun* (The faithful are brothers).

Because they indicate collective solidarity, unity of interests and strong community bonds, the plural forms of sibling terms, unlike other descent terms, cut across status groups and hierarchical differentiations. President Nasser of Egypt used to address the people as *ikhwa, ikhwan* or *akhawat* (the plural forms of *akh* and *ukht*), and many of his folowers and supporters referred to him reciprocally as *akh* Gamal (Gamal being his first name). Just as Nasser saw himself as a collective symbol of national and Islamic brotherhood, his admirers and supporters saw him as the embodiment of their collective will—hence the usage of sibling terms across hierarchic differentiation. By contrast, President Sadat, who saw himself as a symbol of authority, used the term *abna'i* (my sons) in addressing the public, thus enhancing the seniority differentiation.

The extension of parent-child terms—namely, *ab* (father), *umm* (mother), *ibn* (son) and *ibna* (daughter)—to non-kin expresses status differentiations without necessarily implying class distinctions. It signifies parentalistic and familial authority, which would be insulting if exchanged between interactors who consider themselves as of strictly equal social status, such as friends and colleagues. This is why an actor addresses or refers to an equal as *ibn* or *ibna* only if he is dissatisfied with his or her performance. Likewise, a boy or a girl may address or refer to an older person as *bi, ba* or *bu* (meaning *abi*) in a mood of anger and disgust if the latter continues to interfere in the former's private affairs. In this context, the term *umm* is never used in the same way as *ab*. Indeed, *umm* is very rarely used in address or reference forms of interaction between non-kin. The usage of parent-child descent terms is so subtle and governed by such intricate nuances of relationships that people avoid these terms in their daily interactions, especially between strangers. Their usage is confined to those relationships that combine the two elements of long association and status differentiation—such as that between teacher and student, employer and employee, chief and kinsman, boss and subordinate or officer and soldier.

The extension of paternal and maternal uncle-aunt terms (*amm, amma, khal, khala*) to non-kin implies formality, politeness, deference and respect. The term *amm* on the father's side and *khala* on the mother's side are the most commonly used for this purpose. They are used to address or refer to people who are of the same age, sex and status as fathers and mothers. It is in this vein that a man's father-in-law is addressed or referred to as *amm*, his wife as *bint amm* and his mother-in-law as *khala*. In Arabic there are no generic terms for nephews and nieces. They are referred to by a combination of elementary descent terms—a nephew is called 'brother's son' or 'sister's son' and a niece is called 'brother's daughter' or 'sister's daughter'. These terms are used only in their kinship context and not by extension: a person addressed as *amm, amma, khal* or *khala* responds by calling the actor by name or by sibling or parent-child terms, depending upon the particular relationship that binds them. All kinship referents that are formed of a combination of elementary terms are governed by the principles of usage that characterize nephews and nieces. These referents include all relations not discussed in the present chapter.

While *khala* (maternal aunt) is used extendedly to address or refer to any woman who is of the same age and status as the mother, *amma* (paternal aunt) tends to be used only in addressing or referring to womenfolk on the father's side who are of the same age and status as the mother. This usage of *amma* occurs irrespective of the genealogical depth or distance that differentiates between kin interactors. In other words, *amma* is used extendedly within the paternal kin, but *khala* is generalized to all forms of interaction between maternal kin and non-kin. In some circles in Lebanon today, the English term aunt, often pronounced *aunti* (my aunt), and the French term *tante*, often pronounced *tanti* (my *tante*), seem to have replaced the usage of *amma* and *khala* in similar interactional situations. 'Aunt' and '*tante*' are often used by a woman to refer to her mother-in-law to induce a favourable friendly atmosphere between two relations which could otherwise be expected to be stern and competitive.

The usage of *khal* (maternal uncle) is somewhat parallel to *amma* (paternal aunt): it is used extendedly to address or refer to maternal male relatives who are of the same age and status as fathers. However, *khal* is also frequently used in non-kin situations to express joking relationships and less serious moods. This usage is quite different from *amm*, which expresses seriousness and respect.

The extension of grandparent terms (*jadd* and *jadda*) to non-kin—used in interactions between the old and the young—implies affection, closeness and a joking mood. In this sense, *jadd* (often pronounced *jiddo* or *iddo*) and *jadda* (often changed into *teita*) are used reciprocally between the old and the young. When used by the young to address or refer directly to the old, they express respect and politeness mixed with closeness and affection. When used self-reciprocally by the old to address or refer to the young, they imply affection mixed with a less serious mood. In other words, an old man or woman who wants to express affection towards a child addresses him or her as *jiddo* or *teita*.

Unlike descent terms, affinal and ritualistic terms are never used by extension to address or refer to non-kin, or reciprocally between interactors. Affinal and ritualistic terms are used only to address or refer to the kinship relation they signify.

The behavioural contents of affinal relationships, as can be deduced from their meanings in Table 3, are loaded with problems of honour, shame, jealousy, competition, avoidance and other personal sensitivities. The usage of kinship terms in extension forms, as established earlier, is governed by the behavioural expectations that characterize interaction between kin themselves. In other words, the extension of terms to non-kin carries with it the behavioural expectations of kinship relations. This means that the extended or reciprocal usage of affinal terms leads to problems of honour and shame and creates an atmosphere of jealousy and avoidance. The use of affinal terms in the possessive case to address or refer to non-kin creates a wide variety of negative reactions. Ritualistic terms, which include *arrab* and *arraba* (godfather/godmother), *ishbin* and *ishbina* (best man/ female equivalent), *rabiba* (father's wife) and *qatriba* (wife's daughter), are subject to the same mode of usage as affinal terms. They are used in direct address and not extendedly or reciprocally. This is not because of the negative reactions they generate, but because of the non-transferable situations in which they are established—the ritual. *Arrab* and *arraba* are established at baptism and *ishbin* and *ishbina* at weddings; *rabiba* and *qatriba* arise out of non-transferable marriage ceremonies. These ritualistic terms are used only by Arab Christians and not by Muslims, for whom weddings and marriages are legal transactions sanctioned by religious law.

The social world around the Arab, whether actor or interactor and whether in conflict or harmony, co-operation or contradiction, can be captured in small, encapsulated family

Table 3: Meaning of Affinal and Ritualistic Terms

Term	Verbal root	Meaning of root	Kinship referent[a]
Affinal terms[b]			
hurma	*harama*	forbid	W
imra'a	*maru'a*	become dignified	W
nasiba	--	luck, fortune	W
nasib	--	luck, fortune	H
zawja	*zawwaja*	pair	W
zawj	*zawwaja*	pair	H
bint amm	--	FBD	W
ibn amm	--	FBS	H
rajul	*rajila*	walk	H
ba'l	(noun)	lord	H
hamu	*hama*	protect	WF, HF
hama	*hama*	protect	WM, HM
kinna	*kanna*	stay	SW
sihr	*sahara*	weld	DH, ZH
silf	*salafa*	make [soil] even	HB
silfa	*salafa*	make [soil] even	HBW
adil	*adala*	balance	WZH
Ritualistic terms			
arrab	*ariba*	increase	godfather
arraba	*ariba*	increase	godmother
ishbin	(Syriac)	--	best man
rabiba	*raba*	increase	FW
qatriba	--	--	WD

a. F = father   b. H = husband
   M = mother   W = wife
   S = son   WF = wife's father
   D = daughter   HM = husband's mother
   B = brother   etc.
   Z = sister

structures. The use of kinship terms in interactional processes
between people of the same or different age, sex, status or filial
generation, and between friends, strangers, neighbours and non-
kin interactors, shows how the passing and the enduring, the

lasting and the ephemeral, is intertwined in recurrent patterns of interaction. These patterns of usage—direct address, reciprocity and extension—are discussed as they take place in a wide variety of social interactions involving kin and non-kin. Status terms are used either to consolidate status differentiations, thus inducing temporarily an atmosphere of mutual trust and confidence, or to express disgust and discontent. The formal use of status terms in direct address expresses respect, politeness and distance; their self-reciprocal use expresses disgust and discontent.

Kinship terms are often used in non-stratified situations of interaction to express formality, seniority, respect and various levels of intimacy. Only descent terms determined by birth are used reciprocally or in extension forms. Affinal and ritualistic terms are used only in direct address as kinship referents and are not extended to non-kin. The behavioural contents of ritualistic or affinal relationships are non-transferable, whereas those implied in descent relationships are transferable. The problems of honour and shame, avoidance and jealousy, competition and authority which are implied in ritualistic and affinal relationships are non-transferable behavioural expectations. Respect, formality, distance, politeness, disrespect, intimacy, closeness, affection, joking relationships, which constitute the behavioural contents of relationships between descent kin, are transferable.

The reciprocal use of descent terms expresses affection, love and intimacy; their extended use expresses the same behavioural contents as the kin relationships they signify. In other words, to address or refer to an outsider as *amm* (paternal uncle) or *ukht* (sister) reflects or generates the behavioural expectations of uncle-nephew, uncle-niece, brother-sister or sister-sister relationships. If descent terms are extended to outsiders who do not share the same age, sex, status, seniority and levels of formality and intimacy as are implied in the kinship referents, they express joking relationships (if between friends) or ridicule and lack of politeness (if between non-friends). To call a girlfriend *khalti* (my maternal aunt) may provoke laughter or perhaps anger, but to address a new female acquaintance in this way is clearly an insult, implying that she is old and unattractive.

3
Family before Marriage

The non-pyramidal image of reality is best expressed in cousin marriage, namely, the marriage of a man to his father's brother's daughter (FBD) (*bint amm*). In some Arab societies, such as in southern Iraq, a man has a 'right' to his FBD and she can only marry someone else if her cousin forfeits his right first.

FBD marriage atomizes society to the bare minimum: it makes it possible for two married brothers to constitute a complete society entirely on their own. In other words, a person may be born, grow up, marry, have children, even seek salvation—salvation in Islam is an individualized relationship between man and God—without linking himself to any external group or structure.

If the world is seen as an extension of family relationships, family culture then takes precedence over everything else including marriage. This is why 'celibacy' in Islam does not preclude one from having a family since it is possible for a man to recognize a child as his without being formally married to the mother. Biology takes precedence over legality—hence, there are no illegitimate children. Children born to women from unknown fathers are considered orphans. This is what is meant by the phrase *al-walad li-l-firash*, meaning literally, 'The child belongs to the bed,' which is an acceptable precept in Islamic law.

Of course, people marry for many different reasons: love, power, politics, property, job, honour, status, spite, or for any combination of these. But this does not explain why FBD marriage is culturally preferred, since these motives do not vary directly with in- or out-marriage.[1] The relatively high incidence of in-marriages, especially of the FBD type, shows that they fit into the general practice of putting family before marriage. Table 4, taken from a survey of 5,368 marriages in the suburbs of Beirut, illustrates the point.[2]

Table 4: Frequency of In- and Out-Marriages in Two Suburbs of Beirut, 1967–69

Relationship between husband and wife	Marriages among Muslims		Marriages among Christians		Total percentage
	No.	%	No.	%	%
No relationship	1,954	61.72	1,742	79.11	68.85
Distant family relations	354	11.18	202	9.17	10.36
Close family relations	509	16.08	185	8.40	12.93
FBD marriage	349	11.02	73	3.32	7.86
Total	3,166	100.00	2,202	100.00	100.00

In FBD marriage, which constitutes around 38.2% of all marriages contracted between close family relations, the relationships which prevail before marriage continue undisturbed afterwards. By marrying a paternal cousin, a man does not create significant new affinal relationships nor does he alter the consanguine relationships he has learned from childhood. In other words, the same relationships to which he learns to accommodate himself at an early age continue undisturbed after he marries his first paternal cousin. In this sense, FBD marriage nullifies the effects of marriage on the intensity of family relationships.

Given the specifically recognized family relationships in Arab society, the practice of marrying the parallel cousin contributes to more harmonious relationships between members of the consanguine group, who instantly become the in-law group as well. In this sense, FBD marriage is analogous to the Chinese custom of marrying a *t'ung-yang-hsi* (daughter-in-law raised from childhood), regarded by Wolf (1968: 864–74) as a Chinese solution to the problem of the incest taboo. By adopting female children who are raised as wives for their adoptive parents' sons, Chinese families socialize their own daughters-in-law, thus helping to preserve domestic harmony. According to Wolf (1968: 871), many Chinese informants spoke of the *t'ung-yang-hsi* marriage as 'less troublesome'. They added that, 'The girl you adopt won't always be saying things to your son,' and that, 'A girl from another family will always get mad when you try to correct her, and then she will say things to her husband and make trouble between him and his parents.'

Likewise, FBD marriage does not create conflict of roles—as marriage within the same nuclear family would do; nor does it create the affinal, but tense relationships associated with out-marriage (Ammar 1954: 196–8). In the case of FBD marriage, the roles of the consanguine group coincide with or take precedence over the roles of in-laws created by marriage. More specifically, the role of the paternal uncle (*amm*) before marriage coincides with the role of father-in-law (also called *amm*) after marriage; the role of the niece (brother's daughter) with the role of daughter-in-law (*kinni*); and the role of the nephew (brother's son) with the role of son-in-law (*sihr*). Likewise, the role of the paternal uncle's wife before marriage coincides with her role as mother-in-law (*hama*) after marriage; and the same thing happens when cousins become husband and wife, or sisters- and brother-in-law.

Paternal Uncle and Father-in-Law

The relationship between paternal uncle and niece is one of strict formality and reserve (Barclay 1964: 114). The uncle is the same stern guardian and disciplinarian with respect to the niece as her father is, but the father guards and disciplines the daughter with an emotional intensity and tenderness the paternal uncle ought not to show. The uncle who shows affection for his niece, especially if she is sexually mature, invites the jealousy and therefore the hostility of her father and his own son: her father, because he may construe this show of affection as an approach to the mother, following the saying, 'If you want the mother, cuddle the child,' or as a move to replace the father as the recipient of the daughter's affections; his son, because the paternal uncle's daughter is a potential mate. Both before and after her marriage, the daughter is supposed to exhibit a sincere affection for her father.

A girl who seeks a man's love before marriage endangers her purity and also betrays her father's right to her love. Marital relationships are not supposed to be passionate, at least initially, for the woman. It shames the father if his daughter seeks the embraces of her husband publicly, or if she confesses her desire for him. A married daughter, even one who claims to have married her husband for love, will refrain from showing affection for him in the presence of her father. She behaves as if she dominates her husband, which gives her father the false impression that his authority has been established over the son-in-law as well.

The father's attitude towards his daughter, especially if she is unmarried, is affectionate but stern. The paternal uncle, on the other hand, is stern but not affectionate. He will retain this attitude even after he has become his niece's father-in-law, in other words, when his son marries her. Although the restrained relationship between father-in-law and daughter-in-law is somewhat relaxed if the former is a paternal uncle (Barclay 1964: 114), any show of affection between them must still be circumspect. Displays of affection between father-in-law and daughter-in-law are immediately suspect: to the mother-in-law, who feels that she alone is entitled to receive her husband's attention; and to the son, who expects his wife to be not only submissive and chaste, but also a combination of lover and fostering mother. The husband's expectation that his wife should be submissive, chaste and maternal conforms to her father's expectations. The conflict of expectation between father and husband is eased by the fact that the married couple restrain their emotions in the presence of the father-in-law, and also that the father is at the same time uncle to his daughter's husband.

As a paternal cousin, the daughter-in-law tends to reduce tension between father and son, and between brothers, particularly once the father has retired and his sons have married. A paternal cousin is said to 'speak the language of the husband's family'. A great part of the tension between father and son builds up as soon as the latter begins to replace the former in work and social life, or when the son marries and sets up a separate, independent household. At the time that the father feels that his authority and position are being gradually taken over by his son, he tends to cling to them more tenaciously, insisting that the son should follow in his footsteps. If the son proves difficult to manage, the father may threaten to disinherit him or may himself retire from work. It is generally believed that the first of these sanctions is adopted by the father if he is a man of means and character, or if he supports his son financially, while the second is preferred if the son supports his father or otherwise controls the resources on which he lives.

This 'tug of war' between father and son is further complicated by the presence of brothers who all vie with one another to earn their father's favour. As the father grows older and his authority over his sons diminishes, the latter all try to pursue their individual interests at the expense of family solidarity. The fact that all sons, regardless of age, status or seniority, are formally entitled to succeed their father and inherit equal shares of his property makes the pursuit of their individual interests potentially uncompromising, and at times full of conflict. The possibility of conflict between brothers, and between them and their father, increases with the marriage of sons to outsiders or distant relatives. This perhaps explains why the incidence of FBD marriage is higher among influential landowning families than among peasants (Peters 1963: 178–9; Cohen 1965: 122). Conflict between brothers who come from notable families weakens them both economically and politically.

'Stranger-wives' in Arab society are, not without reason, reputed to be responsible for strife between father and son, and brother and brother. They are thought of as 'enemies inside the house'. Such a wife will inevitably be more concerned with the interests of her husband and children (her immediate family) than with the maintenance of her husband's family solidarity. In order to serve the interests of her immediate family, the stranger-wife may employ a variety of devices. She may refuse to serve her father-in-law, who, as he grows older, needs an increasing amount of attention which his wife (the mother-in-law) is reluctant to provide. After the marriage of her son, the mother-in-law tends to neglect her ageing husband and competes with her daughter-in-law for the favours of her son who will provide for her own old age. The stranger-wife may also reveal the family's secrets to outsiders, which shames her husband and reflects on his capacity to control her. These sanctions are not normally employed by a paternal female cousin. If she fails to serve her father-in-law, she fails in her obligations towards her uncle, seen as the equivalent (*badil*) of her father; and if she reveals the family's secrets, she shames her own family. As a wife, the paternal cousin keeps the family's secrets, guards its reputation, and puts pressure on her husband to continue obeying his father and to be on good terms with his brothers (her cousins). She fulfils these obligations and services so judiciously that the incidence of nuclear families living in three-generation households, composed of father and married son or sons, is noticeably higher among families where the spouses are paternal cousins (Table 5). To be exact, the incidence of such families in the suburbs of Beirut which were studied amounts to 11% among those who marry paternal cousins, 4% among those who marry traceable relatives, 3% among those who marry untraceable relatives and 4% among those who marry outsiders.

Table 5: Type of Marriage by Three-Generational Household Composed of Father and Married Son(s)[a]

Kinship connection between wife and husband	Total no. of nuclear families	Nuclear families living in households composed of father and married sons	
		No.	%
None	3,696	148	4.0
Untraceable family relationships	556	15	2.7
Traceable family relationships	694	26	3.7
FBD	422	47	11.1
Total	5,368	236	4.4

a. Data for this table were collected in two suburbs of Beirut from 1967 to 1969.

FBD marriage does not qualitatively change the relationship between paternal uncle and niece, nor does it alter that between uncle and nephew. In other words, the relationship between paternal uncle and nephew after marriage remains one of respect and mutual defence against strangers (Rosenfeld 1968: 474–8). Fathers-in-law and sons-in-law, like paternal uncles and nephews, are social partners. They share the same status, provide mutual support for each other (*sihri sanad dhahri*) and co-operate in time of conflict. Nevertheless, as in-laws, nephews and uncles do not interact very frequently. They belong to different age groups and normally live in separate houses. The little interaction that takes place between them is restricted to social activities. Because brothers have equal shares in their father's estate, and because each tends to manage his share independently, especially after the death of the father, the uncle-nephew relationship, unlike the father-son relationship, is free of common ownership of property, and therefore of the tensions which may result from conflicting economic interests. The nephew's rights to the property of his paternal uncle, when the two men become in-laws, are often settled at the time of marriage. It is true that many uncles provide financial assistance for their nephews, and vice versa; but this is understood to be merely help, which entitles neither to lay legal claims upon the property of the other.

Although the nephew protects the honour (*satr al-ird*) of the uncle by marrying his daughter, he nevertheless deprives the uncle of his daughter's love. Thus the uncle has an ambivalent attitude towards his daughter's marriage. In order to avoid gossip (there is always considered to be something wrong with an unmarried girl of marriageable age), he likes to see his daughter married at the earliest opportunity, yet her marriage deprives him of her love. This feeling of deprivation on the part of the father is greatly eased, though not eliminated, if his daughter marries a nephew. A nephew would be more understanding than an outsider of his uncle's fatherly emotions.

Paternal Uncle's Wife and Mother-in-Law

Much of the traditional conflict between mother-in-law (*hama*) and daughter-in-law (*kinni*) is derived from the fact that they work for opposed interests. While it is in the mother-in-law's interest to keep the family together under the authority of the father (her husband), it is in the daughter-in-law's interest to split the extended family and establish for herself an independent household under the authority of her own husband (the son). In order to perpetuate the authority of the father, after the marriage of the son, the mother-in-law tries to keep the interests of her married son subordinate to those of the family. One way of keeping the married son subordinate is for his mother to 'master' the daughter-in-law, either by supervising her conduct or by controlling the domestic work of the family. The mother-in-law's control over the daughter-in-law demonstrates to the son that his mother's presence in his house, or his presence in his father's house, is necessary if he is to have peace of mind regarding the management of the house and the conduct of his wife.

In the case of FBD marriage, however, mother-in-law and daughter-in-law do not pursue their individual interests too stridently, and this reduces the ill-feeling between them, sometimes eliminating it altogether. In the first place, no woman can use the same severe sanctions against a disobedient niece as she could against a stranger daughter-in-law. She cannot, for example, threaten to ostracize a cousin, because the latter could draw as much support from the adult males of the family as a mother-in-law could, particularly if the mother-in-law herself is an outsider. As a daughter-in-law, the paternal cousin pays the price of the support she receives by subordinating her immediate family's interests to the interests of the extended family.

This does not mean that families who marry cousins remain structurally integrated; indeed, fission occurs, but when it does, it results from the opposed interests of men, not of women. In contrast to out-marriage, FBD marriage seems to nullify the effects women may have upon the division of the extended family into smaller units. Likewise, the customary rule of avoidance between mother-in-law and son-in-law, which may strain relationships between mother and daughter, is somewhat relaxed in the case of FBD marriage. The main reason for the avoidance of mother-in-law by son-in-law, or vice versa, is that any intensive interaction between them may suggest to the former's husband the presence of an illicit relationship, sexual or otherwise. Partly because of sympathy for the daughter, who, according to both Islamic law and Arab custom, seldom receives as many favours from the father as does the son, and partly out of fear that her daughter may be ill-treated by the son-in-law, the mother-in-law tends to treat the latter very generously. 'She [the mother-in-law] cooks good food for him, speaks sincerely about him before other women, and provides his children with gifts and services.'

Suspicious of this generous treatment, the father-in-law asks his wife to reduce her show of affection for the son-in-law and subsequently for her daughter. His request is based, in part, upon the suspicion that the son-in-law competes with him for his wife (the mother-in-law) as much as he (the father-in-law) competes with the son-in-law for the love of his daughter, the latter's wife. This suspicious feeling is aggravated if the in-laws are of comparable age, and therefore mutually attractive sexually. In the case of FBD marriage, however, much of this suspicious feeling on the part of the father-in-law is suppressed. As a paternal uncle, the father-in-law uses his authority not only to control his wife (the mother-in-law) and therefore to be reassured of her loyalty, but also to control his nephew (the son-in-law). Besides, if two brothers marry two paternal parallel cousins, the mother-in-law of the second generation would also be a *khala* (mother's sister) (Fig. 7), and between the *khala* and the sister's son, as the son-in-law, there will be no such rule of avoidance (Barclay 1964: 133).

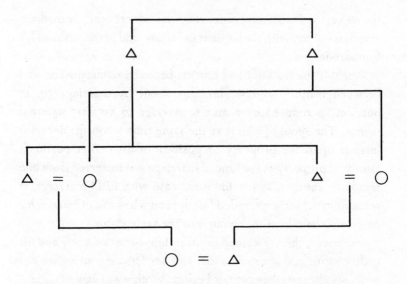

Figure 7: Marriage of Parental Parallel Cousins by Brothers

Parallel Cousins as In-Laws

The jealousy and tension between sisters-in-law, and between brothers-in-law (Rosenfeld 1968: 797), is derived from the fact that one regards the other as a stranger-intruder who, after marriage, becomes entitled to share in the family's fortune and position. Just as a wife may receive bride-wealth from the husband's family, a husband may receive part of the wife's family property by inheritance. Socially, also, marriage equalizes the position of the wife's family with that of the husband's, which, in itself, creates tension, especially if the two families are unequal in social standing. If the husband refuses to associate publicly with his brothers-in-law, or the wife with her sisters-in-law, the spouses will inevitably lose the in-laws' friendship, trust and company. For a wife to lose the company of her sisters-in-law, and for the husband that of his brothers-in-law, has serious consequences in Arab society, where the rules of segregation of the sexes are publicly observed, i.e. where the immediate associates of the wife are her sisters-in-law, and of the husband his brothers-in-law.

Much of the jealousy and tension between sisters-in-law and between brothers-in-law, brought about by marriage to an outsider, is reduced by a man's marriage to his first paternal cousin. The spouse (who is at the same time a cousin) does not intrude upon the property or position of his or her partner's family. If property at the time of marriage is transferred from one family to another, as is seldom the case with FBD marriage, it remains in the same extended family; and when a man marries his paternal cousin he is marrying into the same status group.

Moreover, the prescribed relationships between a boy and his male cousins and between a girl and her female cousins are not seriously altered when cousins become brothers-in-law or sisters-in-law. Cousins of the same age or sex, like brothers- or sisters-in-law, visit each other, enjoy each other's company, gossip, joke and tease. They defend one another in public, stand together against strangers and praise one another's social accomplishments. No doubt there is rivalry between them, particularly between those who venture to lead the others or establish supremacy over them, but this is rivalry between people who are structural and social equals and who enjoy high personal standing. It is 'rivalry within the same house', and is suppressed in public.

Whereas relationships between cousins of the same age and sex are informal, those between cousins of different ages and the opposite sex are formal. Informal interaction between cousins of the opposite sex is strictly avoided, particularly if it suggests sexual attraction; if continued, it would offend the code of modesty for women and subsequently tarnish the honour of men. Likewise, any informal interaction between in-laws of the opposite sex, i.e. between sisters- and brothers-in-law, would expose them to ridicule and is therefore avoided.

Cousins as Husband and Wife

When a girl marries an outsider she has to adjust her ways to those of his family, and when a man marries an outsider he faces a dilemma. Whereas marriage enables him to demonstrate his manliness and to achieve full adult status, it brings into the family an outside element (the wife) who may cause conflict with his father, mother and brothers. But when a man marries his uncle's daughter, he is contributing to the continuity of the same family relationships that existed before the marriage. Here consanguine relationships fit harmoniously into or take precedence over affinal ones, so that the only necessary serious adjustment to be made after marriage is that between husband and wife. The fact that a man's wife is the daughter of his own paternal uncle makes this adjustment easier.

Paternal cousins of the opposite sex rarely interact with each other intimately, particularly if they are potential marriage partners. Yet despite this lack of interaction, they are well informed about each other's character, temperament, tastes and general reputation in the community. The father's brother's son (FBS) gathers information about his FBD from his sisters and her brothers; the FBD, on the other hand, gets similar information from her brothers and his sisters. Since they may be living in the same compound or neighbourhood, and because the rules of segregation between the sexes are not observed by them in private, cousins of marriageable age see each other relatively frequently and exchange smiles, greetings and formal conversations about family affairs. At the same time, they avoid informal talk, gossip, jokes, or gestures that might suggest mutual desire or sexual attraction. They do so not only because they are preferential marriage partners, but also because the nephew, in the absence of the paternal uncle or the uncle's son, assumes responsibility for the conduct of the uncle's daughter (his cousin) which is endangered if she displays open sexual attraction. In Muslim Arab society, sexual attraction and informal relationships between members of the opposite sex are cultural synonyms; hence, the avoidance of informality between cousins of the opposite sex. In this context, marrying outside the group can be seen to oppose kinship obligations in two ways: first, it creates ties with an out-group which may lead to tense affinal relationships; second, if a woman behaves passionately towards her husband in public, it may tarnish the honour of her father.

The formality that is proper between cousins of the opposite sex continues after they marry and become husband and wife. Manliness requires that a man should dominate his wife sexually; and sexual domination, when it is successfully accomplished, requires that the wife should appear chaste, incapable of sexual desire and even uninterested in intercourse.[3] I was told by an old woman in Chiyah (Lebanon) that, 'A good wife never denies intercourse to her husband whenever he desires it.' According to tradition, however, offering intercourse is not equivalent to a show of love. If a woman loves her husband, she is afraid to show it lest she offend his sense of propriety. The ideal wife, it follows, is difficult to arouse and acts only as a passive partner for her husband's pleasure. Her aim in intercourse is the bearing of children.

From this point of view, FBD marriage helps husband and wife to achieve their expected roles. Sexual desire between cousins is deliberately suppressed. Cousins cautiously avoid passion or desire lest they violate the rules of modesty which, as cousins, they should observe. The wife's expectation of sexual satisfaction after marriage, and the husband's expectation of establishing his potency, are accordingly ignored. Failure on the part of the wife to respond positively to the husband's advances, and on the part of the husband to arouse the wife, may be considered marriage norms. When cousins marry, the husband's expected demonstration of his potency and manliness, and the wife's anticipated satisfaction, are forsaken with the aim of achieving modesty.

It is my impression, however, that the suppression of sexual desire after marriage, while favouring the modesty of the wife, negates the potency of the husband, which is considered necessary for the demonstration of manliness. This is where marriage to outsiders or distant relatives strengthens the husband's position. A man who marries an outsider is better able to demonstrate his manliness for the simple reason that he is less concerned about his wife's modesty. So it appears that the achievement of potency and manliness by a man is in direct contrast to the requirements of modesty for women.

A man who marries his FBD suppresses the individual interests of his immediate family and risks his reputation for manliness. A few people have indicated to me that, 'A manly man never marries his cousin.' 'The person who does so is often overwhelmed by family interests,' they say; and, it may be added, by harmonious family relationships as well. Harmonious family relationships can only be achieved at the expense of the interests and independence of individual family members. 'Family relationships dwarf the child and chain people together,' are comments I heard repeatedly in Beirut. To preserve family solidarity, the members must suppress their individual interests. This is difficult to achieve in Arab families, where individual rights to property, power and honour are sanctioned by law and custom. One of the responsibilities of a father, or whoever has authority in the family, is to try to subdue the petty intrigues that adults resort to in an attempt to free themselves from family obligations. Thus, not surprisingly, the verbal root *khalafa* in Arabic, which means 'to succeed', can also mean 'to take from the back', i.e. to conspire (Mas'ud 1964: 639).

FBD Marriage and In-Marriage

The indiscriminate use of the word 'family' in the sociological literature on Arab society glosses over the complexity of its inner organization and the intricate relationships that bind its individual members together. Expressions such as 'family honour', 'family property' and 'family power' are used as if the family actually had honour, property and power. This is further complicated by the fact that the word *a'ilat* (family) can be used to mean a nuclear family, an extended family, a lineage and a clan. As a collective body, the family has neither honour, property nor power—these are the properties of individuals. The sense of *ird* (honour), for example, is the property of the father and the brother. Since women (wife-mother, sister-daughter) are themselves considered the *ird* of men, they have no *ird* of their own. Moreover, paternal uncles and nephews become the protectors of the *ird* only in the absence of fathers and brothers. Property and power also concern individuals in the family and, according to custom, these are often, although not invariably, the concern of the father.

Likewise, the overtly recognized roles and relationships between members of the same family are identified by specific relations—namely, the godparents, uncles and aunts on the mother's side, and these plus the parallel cousins and the uncle's wife on the father's side (Fig. 8). I shall call these relationships 'specific' (ego-centric).

On the other hand, the relationship between a man and (a) the wife of his maternal uncle, (b) the husbands of his paternal and maternal aunts, (c) the children of his maternal uncle and (d) the children of his paternal and maternal aunts are never clearly identified. In Lebanon, these relationships are described in very general terms which can be used, by extension, to refer to outsiders as well. They include the following: *qarib* (close), *awlad amm* (cousinly), *a'iliya* (familial), *akhawiya* (brotherly), *nafs al-shai*

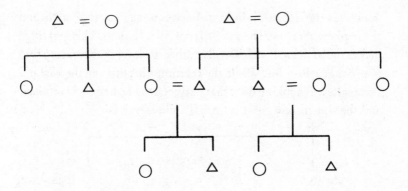

Figure 8: Specific Relationships

(same thing) and *nafs al-a'ila* (same family). I shall call these relationships 'general' (socio-centric).

The fact that people make clear distinctions between specific and general family relationships suggests that the definition of in-marriage used in most of the literature (at least in reference to Arab society) is invalid. In-marriage is not simply any marriage within the same kin group. Based on the overtly recognized specific family relationships (Fig. 8), in-marriage would then include cross-cousin and parallel-cousin marriages only. By defining in-marriage in this way, the incidence of these marriages, which amounts to 83% of all in-marriages (see Table 4), would become more meaningful.

Nevertheless, the argument put forward for FBD marriage here cannot be generalized to include MZD marriage[4] or cross-cousin marriages: although the latter are biologically similar, they differ from FBD marriage socially, in terms of specific family relationships. If a man marries his MBD, only one role, that of the paternal aunt (*amma*), would coincide with the role of mother-in-law (*hama*). The paternal aunt commands the respect of, and exercises control over, the niece, just as a mother-in-law

67

does over the daughter-in-law. Between the maternal uncle and the nephew there will be a conflict of roles (Fig. 9). This marriage makes the maternal uncle (*khal*) a father-in-law, thus creating two non-congruent roles. While the relationship between the *khal* and the nephew is a joking one, that between the father-in-law (*amm*) and the son-in-law (*sihr*) is formal and reserved.

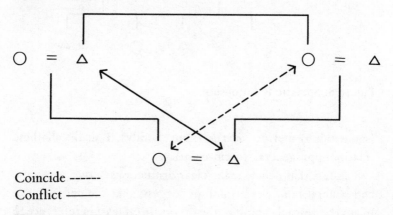

Coincide ------
Conflict ———

Figure 9: MBD Marriage

Other relationships, such as those between the nephew and the wife of the maternal uncle, or between the niece and the husband of the paternal aunt, or between cross-cousins, would become strictly affinal. They neither coincide with, nor take precedence over the existing family relationships before marriage. Affinal relationships require a variety of readjustments and are full of tense and conflicting interests.

Likewise, the marriage of a man to his MZD or FZD establishes a variety of new affinal relationships unconnected to those that existed before marriage. MZD marriage establishes affinal relationships between a man and the husband or children of his maternal aunt. At the same time, this marriage makes his maternal aunt (*khala*) his mother-in-law (*hama*), which reduces the expected tension between her and her niece (as her daughter-in-law), and also tempers the rigidity of the rule of avoidance between her and her nephew (as her son-in-law). Besides, the fact that two sisters have married their children to each other contributes to the continuity of intimate relationships between them, especially if they are married to stranger-husbands.

On the other hand, FZD marriage creates new affinal ties between the groom and the husband and children of his paternal aunt, and between the bride and the wife and children of her maternal uncle. In addition, this marriage makes the maternal uncle (*khal*) a father-in-law (*amm*) to the bride, and the groom's paternal aunt (*amma*) becomes his mother-in-law. The relationship between the *khal* and his niece is essentially a joking one, unless they belong to the same age group, in which case joking between them offends the modesty of the niece. If they do belong to the same age group, their relationship becomes formal. However, since men in Arab society tend to marry girls younger than themselves, it is unlikely for the *khal* to belong to the same age group as the niece whom his son is marrying. The relationship, therefore, between the *khal* and his niece, at the time his son is marrying her, is expected to be informal. When the *khal* becomes a father-in-law (*amm*), his role accordingly becomes ambivalent. As a *khal* he ought to respond informally to his niece, but as an *amm* (father-in-law) he is expected to be formal when his niece becomes his daughter-in-law; hence, the conflict of roles (Fig. 10).

Unlike the relationship between the *khal* and his niece, which is altered by age, that between the *amma* (paternal aunt) and her nephew is altered by the marriage of the *amma*, especially if she bears children. Before her marriage, the *amma* is a close relative who cuddles, plays with and occasionally disciplines her nephew. After her marriage, however, she becomes distant and reserved. Otherwise, she would invite the jealousy of her husband, who

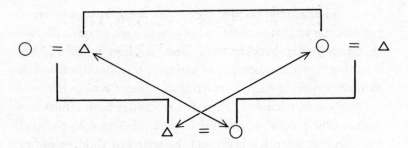

Figure 10: FZD Marriage

would prefer to see her cuddle his own children. The role of the *amma* after the marriage of her nephew to her daughter would then correspond to the original role of mother-in-law, i.e. that of avoiding the son-in-law.

In contrast to FZD, MBD and MZD marriages, FBD marriage does not establish any new affinal relationships. The same specifically recognized family relationships between a man and his consanguine relatives before marriage continue after he marries his paternal cousin. It is in this sense that FBD marriage contributes to harmonious family relationships: the same family relationships to which people learn to accommodate at an early age continue after they marry and reach adulthood. Putting family before marriage is one way of constructing a person's *khanat* for protection and manipulation.

4
The Trap of Kinship:
The Etiquette of Bargaining

If interaction is a game, it is played with rules, to win or lose, not to establish justice. What matters in a game is to win, right or wrong. The variations of mood expressed in kinship terms lend themselves to manipulation, especially in market transactions and politics.

Treating the world as brothers and sisters, uncles and aunts, nieces and nephews, or as cousins is an instrumental strategy meant to affect behaviour and induce favourable dispositions, sometimes through love and affection and sometimes through anger and disgust. Nowhere is this better illustrated than in bargaining techniques, where buyers and sellers confront each other with opposed economic interests.[1] They may try to soften their opposed positions by the use of kinship terms that generate closeness or, on the contrary, use terms that express distance, in which case the deal is called off. While closeness creates trust, enabling buyers and sellers to conclude their deal sucessfully and perhaps develop lasting clientele relationships, distance creates conflict and subsequently no transaction takes place.

In economic terms, markets in which bargaining occurs are characterized by a flexible price policy, by the non-standardization of weights, measures and goods, and by the lack of a mass media that can inform both buyer and seller about the supply-and-demand situation. Mass production and consumption, standardized weights and measures, the separation of the producer from the distributor, the control of production and distribution that produces a continuous balance between supply and demand, the presence of an effective mass media that can publicize current prices, and finally, the impersonal relationships that exist in these markets—these are all factors that restrict bargaining. But they do not determine it. Even when these factors dominate, as in North America, Western Europe and Japan, bargaining still occurs, although perhaps only in relation to certain types of goods and services, such as used cars, real estate, labourers' wages and professors' salaries. Labour unions and management in the United States have instituted bargaining procedures in order to reach the peaceful settlement of disputes.

Although market and social conditions may favour bargaining, as in the *suqs* (markets) of the Middle East, bargaining may still be precluded on the basis of the social standing of the bargainer. People of honour and prestige in this part of the world do not bargain, even when they know that the goods they are buying are overpriced. This is because bargaining, like penny-pinching, does not accord with prestige. The ability to pay appears to be linked to a person's honour, whether expressed in hospitality towards strangers, in pre-eminence among equals or in gaining precedence over traders by deliberately buying their overpriced goods without bargaining. A Beirut carpet-trader commented to me in 1967, 'Notables do not bargain,' adding regretfully, 'It is difficult to distinguish notables from commoners these days; everybody bargains.' In brief, people bargain when they confront each other not only as opposed interests in a market, but also as social equals interacting on a free unbounded basis, one that is free from social obligations.

Bargaining techniques open with standardized expressions of

respect, affection and common interest and trust. The seller welcomes the buyer into his shop, addressing him by kinship terms as a mark of respect or affection. Consider the following bargaining episode as recorded in Beirut in 1967:

Seller: Welcome, brother (*akh*)! I haven't seen you for a long time.

Buyer: Why? I do come here, brother, from time to time.

Seller: You [come]. . .from south Lebanon?

Buyer: Certainly, from the family of H.

Seller: Oh. . . I know some of the H's; they run for elections.

Buyer: Politics is for politicians.

Seller: My shop is yours—desire and order.

Buyer: You are the lord. I simply want to buy some clothes for my children.

Seller: What clothes?

Buyer: Ready-made. Good quality and cheap.

Seller: Shirts, underwear, trousers?

Buyer: Socks and underwear for children of 7, 9 and 10.

Seller: Best quality. . . Italian-made.

Buyer: But [they are] mixed with nylon.

Seller: Slightly.

Buyer: Approximately how much?

Seller: Pay as much as you want. We shall not disagree.

Buyer: Mr M. told me that this shop is the most reliable.

Seller: I've known him [Mr M.] for a long time. He's a friend of yours? For your sake, pay LL3 [3 Lebanese pounds] for each of these [items of underwear], and LL1.75 for these [each pair of socks].

Buyer: Isn't that a little expensive for me, brother?

Seller: By God, brother, it's only for you.

Buyer: The sum is LL32. I'll give you LL30.

Seller: God is generous. That's cost price. Please pay. God will open it [fortune] up for me. Enjoy wearing them.

'Welcome, brother!' Kinship terms indicate respect if used in their extended meaning: a seller who addresses a buyer or vice versa as 'brother' intends to generate an atmosphere of trust and equality. While bargaining, buyers and sellers hardly use a sentence without punctuating it with kinship terms. 'Brother', 'sister', 'father', 'mother', 'uncle', 'aunt', 'family' and 'relatives' are all used to affect behaviour and create a relaxed, comfortable mood or, reversibly, to break off relations. If the buyer's social standing is higher than that of the seller, the latter will address him by a title such as *shaikh, bey* or *janab hadirtak*, indicating that a formal relationship exists between them. In this situation, informality and the mutual trust it tends to create are unnecessary, since men of high social status do not bargain.

As soon as the buyer asks for a commodity and inquires about its price, the seller will respond vaguely:

Between us, 'uncle' (*amm*), there is no difference; we share the same interest. Price is not what pleases me; what pleases me is to find out what pleases you. Pay as much as you want. Brothers do not disagree on price. For you it is free—it is a gift.

These expressions, signifying common interest and trust, symbolize the economic behaviour of corporate family groups, whether nuclear or extended. No buyer in the Middle East, however, takes these words seriously; he or she will subsequently insist on being given a final price, not necessarily the lowest. With a show of hesitancy, the seller suggests a price and starts to advertise his goods, especially the imported ones. Imported goods enable the seller to strike a better deal, for the simple reason that their price and quality are less known to the buyer than the locally manufactured goods. In this sense, restrictions on foreign trade inevitably reduce the seller's profits, as the Lebanese traders both in Lebanon and in West Africa complain.

In any bargaining situation, the seller aims to affect the buyer's choice behaviour, which he can do by assessing the latter's status and appreciating his or her customs and values. Shopkeepers in Lebanon are extraordinarily perceptive of people's accents, dress, cleanliness, names and the way these correlate with specific backgrounds. Names, for example, often suggest sect and clan membership; accents and dialects suggest regional and sometimes village membership; dress and extent of cleanliness suggest class membership. Like their counterparts in Lebanon, the Lebanese traders in West Africa recognize a variety of native tongues, tribal divisions and status symbols, which they manipulate to affect the choice behaviour of Africans. The seller uses such key associations to link the commodity to the buyer's background in an effort to show him that other people of his status consume the same goods by citing specific incidents—for example, a Beirut carpet trader told an American customer who wanted to buy a Bokhara carpet in 1967:

I deal mostly with Americans and with the people of the American University of Beirut. They like my carpets and my prices. See the postcards they send me; all are pleased with my dealings. All of my American customers are happy with my Bokhara; this colour [golden red] goes with American furniture.

While praising the seller for his reliability, the buyer, in his turn, insists on being treated as a permanent client, rather than as a transient customer. And to reinforce his insistence, he refers to the seller's friends and relatives as having recommended the shop. Meanwhile, he tries to establish the final price and the quality of the commodity without offending the seller, for offending the seller terminates bargaining without concluding the sale:

Buyer: Are you sure this suit is made in Italy?

Seller: What's that? What are we doing here, oh 'uncle' (*khal*)? Aren't we trading? We're not playing.

Buyer: It [the suit] looks as if it's made here [Lebanon].

Seller: Are we lying then?

Buyer: God knows.

Seller: Don't buy. Drive on (*yalla*). See you some other time.

'Oh *khal*' (maternal uncle) in this context expresses anger that puts an end to negotiations. The buyer should never directly query the commodity's quality, as this may show ignorance on his part which would expose him to cheating and perhaps ridicule. Indirect inquiry, by comparing the commodity with a familiar one, is a more appropriate procedure—while neither offending the seller nor exposing the buyer's ignorance, it helps establish the real quality of the commodity:

Buyer: How does this shirt compare with Arrow [shirts]?

Seller: Arrow shirts are a little better but more expensive.

Buyer: Arrow shirts are sold for LL15 each, and you want LL13 for this one?

Seller: Arrow is smarter, but this shirt will last longer.

Buyer: LL11.

Seller: Take it for 12.

Buyer: 11½.

Seller: OK, take it—I haven't sold anything today.

In pursuing the bargaining, the seller then asks the buyer to price the commodity and declare the amount of money he intends to pay. If the buyer were to agree to this request, he would, first, be restricting his own power of choice, and, second, be giving the seller the initiative in calling off or continuing with the bargaining. Instead, the seller asks the buyer to price his own commodities, thus gaining the initiative and warding off the possibility of being insulted if the seller abruptly decides to end the bargaining. When the seller sets a price, the buyer immediately declares that it is expensive and pretends to leave the shop—an act that often triggers the seller into constantly dropping his price until agreement is finally reached. Agreeing on a final price, however, does not mean that the sale is concluded. Many buyers test the prices by bargaining in one shop and then buying their goods in another. This behaviour is so common, in both Africa and the Middle East, that shops situated at the entrance to a *suq* are considered less profitable than those situated in the centre. These shops, a shopkeeper in Rabat (Morocco) complained, are 'rich in bargaining but poor in selling'.

When a sale has been agreed, the seller may refuse to be paid on the spot, insisting on extending credit to the buyer; from the buyer's point of view, this is regarded as a gesture of trust, but for the seller, it is a move to win the buyer's custom. Upon concluding the deal, the seller may say to the buyer, 'Pay nothing now; you are a member of the family.' Few buyers take this gesture seriously and most insist on paying immediately. Middle Easterners and Africans take pride in being trusted by their shopkeepers, meaning that they are 'men of their word' (they never delay or deny their debts); they command respect and are comfortably off.

More complicated still are the bargaining techniques that centre on the confusion of husband–wife relationships, especially common among the Lebanese traders in West Africa, or father-son relationships, common in the Middle East. In West Africa, where Lebanese wives may tend shops with their husbands, a shopkeeper's wife, in a show of defiance, will offer the customer a lower price than the one her husband has suggested, leaving the customer certain that her price is indeed minimal. This certainty is reinforced not only by the husband's initial reluctance to sell the

77

commodity for the price suggested by his wife, but also by his scolding her, even to the extent of using abusive language. In West Africa, such language is a serious offence, often tried before a court. Africans do not consider it as a joke, therefore, when a Lebanese husband scolds his wife: 'You, a wife! Ha. . .ha!. . .[I rue] the day I married you!'

In West Africa, this pretend squabble between shopkeeper and wife is performed with such skill that I myself, although Lebanese, have been taken in by it. In Lebanon no merchant of 'honour' allows his wife to work in the shop; the wife's role as a bargaining associate is played by the merchant's sons or brothers. To counterbalance this husband-wife or father-son association in bargaining, customers in both Africa and the Middle East often go shopping accompanied by friends or relatives, who in their turn provide support for the buyer.

The bargaining techniques of underpricing (under the market price) and overpricing (over the market price) are also occasionally employed by Lebanese traders in West Africa. If a buyer starts to check prices at random, without showing interest in any specific commodity, the seller then deliberately underprices his merchandise, which makes it difficult for the buyer to shop elsewhere. But when the buyer comes back to the same shop to buy what he needs, realizing that prices elsewhere are relatively higher, the seller refuses to sell him the goods for less than the current price, pretending that he was insulted when the buyer initially distrusted him. According to one Lebanese trader in West Africa, however, African customers prefer to shop where they have been treated, at least initially, with trust.

Overpricing is particularly noticeable among the Lebanese diamond dealers in Sierra Leone, who act as middlemen between African diamond miners and De Beers, a foreign-owned company that has the monopoly on marketing diamonds outside the country. The miners are not allowed to sell their diamonds directly to the company unless they possess, in addition to a miner's licence, a dealer's licence, which cost £500 in the mid-1960s.

While inspecting a 'diamond lot' to buy, a Lebanese dealer will try to undervalue the gems by overemphasizing any defects such as cracks, spots and yellowish colours. If the customer (i.e. the miner) proves to be tactful in bargaining but incompetent in diamond pricing (which is interpreted by the dealer to mean that the customer's aim, at least at this stage, is just to price his gems, not to sell them), the dealer then manoeuvres against the customer by offering him an over-the-market price. As expected by the dealer, the customer who is uninformed of prices will refuse to sell his 'lot', hoping to get a better price elsewhere. When he approaches other dealers, however, and discovers that their prices are lower than those suggested by the first dealer, the customer inevitably returns to the first dealer. Here he is disappointed to learn that even this dealer will not buy the lot for the same price he himself suggested earlier.

The dealer, of course, justifies his refusal to buy the lot on the grounds that the customer is unworthy of 'good treatment', because he was distrustful of the dealer when he offered to buy the gems for an over-the-market price in the beginning. Since overpricing makes it difficult for the customer to sell his gems elsewhere, the Lebanese dealers in Sierra Leone refer to the technique of overpricing as 'burning the diamond lot', which means it can only be resold by scattering its individual gems over other lots.

Not all bargaining techniques follow the procedures discussed above. They vary with price and the repeated consumption of commodities. With regard to price, Table 6 shows how bargaining time varies with price: the higher the average price (meeting competition), the longer the average bargaining time.

The range of time, however, indicates that certain bargaining

Table 6: Average and Range of Prices of 42 Sales as they Vary with Average and Range of Bargaining Time[a]

Type of commodity	No. of sales	Range of prices in LL	Average price in LL	Range of time in mins. and secs.	Average time in mins. and secs.
Carpets	7	500.00–5,000.00	1,765.00	100′–09′	54′
Carpets	12	25.00– 200.00	146.00	45′–10′	36′
Clothes	18	1.00– 25.00	9.22	07′–02′	05′ 10″
Foodstuffs	5	0.25– 8.00	1.88	03′–12″	00′ 41″

a. Data for this table were collected in Beirut in 1967.

episodes, especially for foodstuffs, may be concluded in a very short period of time. Repeated consumption tends to reduce the bargaining time, or even to eliminate bargaining altogether once a regular patronage has been established between merchant and customer. The data collected on bargained and unbargained sales show that staples such as sugar, bread, oil and meat involve the least bargaining because of their repeated consumption, regardless of whether or not their prices have been arbitrarily fixed by local authorities. Indeed, bargaining over any commodity takes place only once, after which the final price becomes customary for the bargaining partners concerned. In this sense, a customer saves time and bargaining if he establishes a lifelong client relationship with those who serve him—masons, carpenters, butchers, shopkeepers, blacksmiths, goldsmiths, barbers and so on. Such lifelong clientship, as a preferred, sometimes inherited, relationship in the Middle East, must not be confused with friendship. Many clients deliberately avoid friendship with tradesmen, who often manipulate these friendships to delay fulfilling their customer's requests, or even to pass off shoddy work. Tradesmen realize that they can convince a friend-client to accept their terms, but they lose a non-friend-client if his own terms are not fulfilled. From the customer's point of view, it is more advantageous, therefore, to be the client of a tradesman, not a friend.

Women are reputed to spend longer over bargaining than men, but this does not mean that they are able to drive better bargains. They simply 'argue a lot'. This is not an inherent tendency in women, as many Middle Eastern traders like to suggest, but a reflection of cultural norms. A seller will rarely discontinue bargaining with a woman, as he might do with a man, as this is considered an act of disrespect; propriety requires that women be shown respect in public. Perhaps more important, however, is the mood of the seller who, irrespective of his age, shows more willingness to bargain with women. His moods with men seem to vary with the time of day. In the afternoons, sellers have less 'spirit' for bargaining; this favours the buyer more than the seller, since, at that time, the latter is tempted to offer final, minimal prices with little or no bargaining.

Does the seller or the buyer profit from bargaining? Table 7 shows that, given the same commodity, bargained sales are less profitable to the seller than unbargained ones, which means that bargaining, on the whole, favours the buyer. The tendency to bargain in the Middle East is therefore reinforced by material gain.

Table 7: Profit per Sale of Bargained and Unbargained Sales[a]

Type of sale	No. of sales	Cost price in LL	Selling price in LL	Total profits in LL	Average profit per sale in LL
Bargained sales	132	5,070	6,160	1,090	8.25
Unbargained sales	211	14,425	17,221	2,696	12.76

a. Data for this table were collected in Beirut in 1967.

In the Middle East, bargaining is not for fun, nor merely for the sake of bargaining.[2] Through the manipulation of cultural norms and symbols, a bargainer, whether seller or buyer, aims to eliminate any suspicion of both commodity and price and establish instead an atmosphere of trust, often leading to client-relationships, and occasionally to friendship. While it is true that 'business tricks', such as overpricing, underpricing and credit, are used, they will not be successful without the initial establishment of trust and through an idiom of trust: kinship terms, polite formulas and the observance of good manners. A bargainer's failure to evoke and manipulate this idiom of trust will eventually lead to the failure of the intended transaction. As long as the concluding of a transaction depends primarily on the establishment of trust in bargaining, trust necessarily takes precedence over the profit motive. Any act of discourtesy expressed in kinship terms, or otherwise, inevitably puts an end to the bargaining.

In bargaining, the social status of the partners involved is at stake. They attempt to neutralize this status by following the strict rules of bargaining etiquette. But bargaining is used not only to neutralize positions, but also to improve them. If either party to the bargain, seller or buyer, is unusually successful in his approach, he earns social recognition among his group by developing the reputation of knowing how to 'handle' people and subsequently affect their choice behaviour. Since success in bargaining is translated into social recognition, seller-bargainers in the Middle East resort to many kinds of polite formulas to affect the economic choice of their partners. These polite formulas are used with such extravagance that many people, especially foreigners, tend to cite them as revealing the 'bazaarish' character of the Levantine. In fact, these formulas form an essential part of the bargaining technique.

The following anecdote indicates how foreigners may misinterpret the rules of bargaining. In order to win a Canadian woman's trust and subsequently affect her economic behaviour, a Beirut carpet trader jokingly suggested that he become her son-in-law. Shocked by this suggestion, the woman nervously took her daughter by the hand and instantly left the shop. The carpet trader complained, 'She didn't even say goodbye!' Affinal kinship terms are never extended to non-kin, whether in Lebanon or, clearly, in Canada.

5
The Manipulation of Equality: The Case of Family Associations

No hierarchy, no kings or castles, queens or horses—like chequers on a *dama* board, human beings are inherently equal. The world of equals is the world of kin. The world, by extension, is made up of kin, real or simulated. Authority and power are then derived by dominating equals, by being first among equals. To be 'first', a leader has to dominate his equals, in other words, his kin. They are grouped in *khanats*, various kinds of social solidarities, for protection.

Family associations are one type of *khanat* that people manipulate to assert their claim to leadership in a changing community where family structures are loose. Whether or not they make it to the top depends entirely upon their personal qualities and skills.[1] The strategy is to try initially to create a 'world' of equals and then seek to become the first among them. The cases discussed below show that the process of structuring a family association is, in itself, an attempt to become 'first'. Before discussing these cases in detail, it is necessary to describe the suburban setting within which these family associations emerged.

The study on which this chapter is based was undertaken in the late 1960s in the southern suburbs of Chiyah and Ghobeire in Beirut. Between 1925 and 1969 Chiyah had grown from a village of 575 households into two separate suburban municipalities (Chiyah and Ghobeire) composed of more than 5,000 households with a population of over 30,000.[2] Although these statistics no longer hold true for 1990, this does not alter the basic cultural argument about the manipulation of family links.

From the mid-1930s onwards rural-to-urban migrants began to settle in the area at an unprecedented rate. Muslim migrants, especially the Shi'a, settled in Ghobeire; Christian migrants, especially the Maronites, settled in Chiyah. This sudden influx of rural-to-urban migrants rapidly turned the two villages into suburbs in the early 1950s. Fields (orange and olive orchards) were sold as building plots for the construction of apartment blocks; new light industries were set up; new occupations and political groups began to emerge; economic opportunities, educational facilities and neighbourhoods all began to take new forms. The two suburbs were indeed undergoing a period of rapid organizational change. It was during this period (the early 1950s) that family associations began to mushroom in the suburbs, especially among the Shi'a.

Family Associations
In 1970, of the 21 officially registered family associations in the suburbs of Chiyah and Ghobeire, only 4 were still operating, and all of them were Shi'a. The rest, 2 Maronite and 15 Shi'a, had ceased to operate. By 'operating' is meant that they have an elected 'cabinet', composed of a president, a secretary and a treasurer. The difference in number between the officially registered associations (21) and the active ones (4) is partly a bureaucratic problem. To register an association, and therefore make it legal, three signatures are required, those of the president, secretary and treasurer. These officials prepare a written statement about the aims of the association, indicating the date and place of its founding, and submit it to the Ministry of Social

Works. If they receive no reply from the ministry within two months, the association then becomes legal. Seeking legal status for the association earns the founders, particularly the president, the reputation of being 'clever' men who understand bureaucratic formalities. Legal status gives the founders an unchallengeable claim, not only over the right to collect membership fees (itself a political act), but also to grant or refuse admission to the association. The only form that opposition can take in the face of a licensed association is to refuse to join. Membership in family associations based on genealogical links is not automatically established the moment an association is founded. By securing legal recognition, the founders simply earn the power to manoeuvre for members.

In his work on the camel-herding bedouin of Cyrenaica (Libya), Peters (1967: 261) writes, 'The lineage model is not a sociological one, but it is a frame of reference used by a particular people to give them a commonsense kind of understanding of their social relationships.' In relation to family associations in Chiyah and Ghobeire, the 'particular person' is the founder of the association who uses genealogical links as a frame of reference to pursue his own individual interests. In this sense, the limits of the association reflect the founder's interests.

Cases of Family Associations

1. In 1953 Michel, the son of Sij'an Ghusn, founded a Maronite family association that aimed to educate the poor, aid the sick and needy, establish a club and strengthen family bonds. Michel abandoned his project only three months after he had begun it. Personal and organizational factors were responsible for his failure. As Yusuf Ghusn put it, 'Michel belonged to the Risha branch, the least notable of the family; he was young and ambitious but did not measure up to the standards of leadership among the Ghusns.' In fact, the Ghusns already had two powerful,

outspoken leaders when Michel decided he also wanted to be one. Michel's failure to establish a family association, however, cannot be explained by lack of personal qualities alone—organizational reasons were also involved.

Those who claimed to be Ghusns were known by four lineage names: Ghusns proper, Rishas, Dahuds and the Khourys. There was agreement that Ghusn, Risha and Eliya had settled in Chiyah together towards the end of the eighteenth century, but disagreement as to whether they were brothers or cousins (see the Ghusns' genealogy, Fig. 11). Those who said that they were brothers insisted that the Ghusns proper, the Rishas (some of whom had changed their family name to Ghusn) and the Eliyas (both those who belonged to the Dahud lineage and the Khourys) were descendants of one ancestor and were therefore entitled to membership in the association. By contrast, those who said that

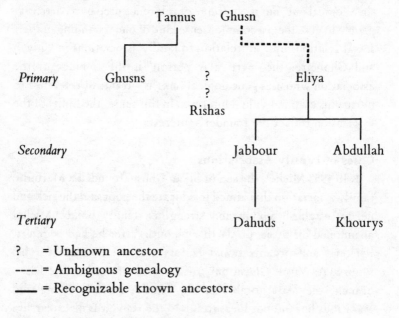

? = Unknown ancestor

---- = Ambiguous genealogy

___ = Recognizable known ancestors

Figure 11: Ghusn Family Tree

Ghusn, Risha and Eliya were cousins insisted that there were no valid grounds to include all these lineages in one association. They argued that the word 'cousin' is a loose term, often used as a cultural idiom, to refer either to genealogical links (and here it is very loose for it may refer to an actual cousin or anybody sharing common descent) or to common residence in the past.

Coming from the Risha branch, itself an offshoot of the Ghusn family, Michel had no chance of playing the role of organizer and bringing the Ghusns together into a single family association. The cynics dismissed his attempt to establish a family association as a manoeuvre to ally himself with the most powerful and numerous family in Chiyah, the Ghusns proper.

2. The other inactive Maronite family association was that of the Iranis, established in 1952 by Alfred al-Irani from the villge of Araiya in the Metn district of Mount Lebanon. The Iranis, who had been living in Chiyah for about four generations and who counted 17 nuclear families, were affiliated to the Kata'ib (the Phalangists), which champions the cause of the Maronites. Because of its relatively small size (17 nuclear families) and because its members engaged in intensive interaction among themselves, the Irani family had no genealogical uncertainties similar to those among the Ghusns. They all traced descent through different ancestors to Yusuf Irani, whom they regarded as the first settler in Chiyah. These two factors—support for the Kata'ib and an established genealogy—were responsible for the fact that the Iranis of Chiyah were members, not initiators, of the family association. Faced with what was accepted as a well-defined genealogy, Alfred al-Irani could not claim to be re-establishing family bonds—they were already well-established. Nor, for that matter, could he claim to be uniting the family into a single political front—they were already united by the Kata'ib. As will be shown later, genealogical disagreements always reflect

political disunity. As a 'foreigner' not even living in Chiyah, Alfred could not possibly hope to use family background to advance his political ambitions. Indeed, his ambition turned out to be economic gain. After meeting twice with the Iranis of Chiyah, Alfred charted a family tree in which he included the Chiyah branch and sold it to them for LL50 a piece. Judging from a photograph, I believe the Irani tree was too neat to be correct. The funds of the Irani association established by Alfred in 1952 ended up in his bank account.

3. The (Shi'a) Khalil family association was first established in Tyre (south Lebanon) in 1921 under the leadership of the late Kadhim al-Khalil, one of the most prominent leaders of the family. In 1970 he was vice-president of the Free Patriots Party founded by President Camille Chamoun on leaving office in 1958. The scope of the association reflected Kadhim's aims at the time. Looking for the widest range of links, real or fictitious, that might tie all the Khalils together, Kadhim traced the origin of the family to none other than Abraham who, in ancient Arabic lore, is called Ibrahim al-Khalil. By doing so, he made it possible for everyone bearing the name Khalil, which is very common among the Shi'a of Lebanon, to join the association. Accordingly, Khalils from the districts of Sidon, Baalbek and Beirut, including Borj al-Brajne and Ghobeire, became eligible for membership, even though no exactly traceable genealogy linked them together. By tracing the origin of the family to Abraham, Kadhim earned the maximal range of potential supporters possible on the basis of descent. Genealogical depth (in lineal terms) means a wider range of collateral relations, and hence, an increase in potential supporters. The reason, therefore, that well-established families have longer genealogies than those of peasants (Peters 1963) is that such genealogies give them a wider range of support and greater freedom of political action.

It was during the French Mandate in Lebanon, and especially between 1925 and 1945, when parliamentary representation was based on large constituencies (all south Lebanon, for example, was one constituency) that such nation-wide links as the Khalil association were of the utmost political importance. Later, especially after independence, when in 1950 electoral constituencies were greatly reduced in size (Tyre alone became a separate constituency), family associations with national links became politically insignificant. By mobilizing the loyalty of the Khalils in Tyre, Kadhim was able, after independence, repeatedly to win the Tyre seat in parliament. Since it was no longer needed, the Khalil family association, with its nation-wide links, was forgotten. Instead, local attempts were made to establish micro-associations, each independent of the other. One such attempt was made in Sidon, another in Ghobeire.

The Ghobeire micro-association first appeared in 1951 under the leadership of Abdulkarim al-Khalil. He belonged to the Mahdi branch, which was by 1970 the most prominent branch of the Khalil family in the suburb. The Mahdi branch traced its descent to al-Hajj Mahdi al-Khalil, said to be one of the descendants of Muhammad al-Khalil, the ancient ancestor who migrated from the village of Shhur (Tyre district) some five centuries ago and settled in the old Shi'a community of Borj al-Brajne. In the middle of the nineteenth century, al-Hajj Mahdi, with six other Khalils (Yusuf, Qasim, Husain, al-Fahl, Jabri and Yahya) who claimed to be the descendants of Muhammad al-Khalil, bought land in what is known today as Ghobeire (then Chiyah) and settled there. These names represented seven different lineages which, though known locally as the Khalayili (plural of Khalil), shared no exact genealogy. Some said that the seven descendants of Muhammad were 'cousins' but disagreed on the actual linkages between them. Others said that they were 'brothers' but, again, disagreed on who was brother to whom.

These seven branches, which included about 281 nuclear families, called themselves 'the old settlers' of Ghobeire in contrast to six other Khalil groups who settled in the suburb after 1925 and were known as 'foreigners'. The latter groups, which counted about 43 nuclear families, came from different villages of Lebanon, one from the Baalbek area and five from the south.

Under Abdulkarim's leadership, the association, which included the old branches only, was torn by internal dissent: every branch had a candidate for the presidency of the association, a candidate for the local government and an independent spokesman. This lack of unity betrayed the aim for which the association was established, namely, to unite the Khalils into a single political front. Abdulkarim gradually lost interest in the association, which continued, for lack of challenge, to have a nominal cabinet until 1969.

In 1969 Ali al-Khalil, a doctor by profession and a Mahdi by lineage, tried to revive the association. Once he was nominated president, Ali invited all the Khalils, old settlers and newcomers alike, to join but in different capacities: the former as participants in the executive council, the latter as members. What prompted Ali to revive the association was the new political challenge the Khalils had to meet after they lost the municipal elections of 1963. The challenge centred around the financing of a sports club established in 1954 under the leadership of Hammoud Khalil for the exclusive use of the seven old branches of the family. This club, though a family enterprise, received continuous subsidies from the municipality at the time the Khalils were in control of it. When the Khalils lost the 1963 elections, they also lost the subsidies for the club. Supporting the club financially became, therefore, a symbol of family solidarity, a way of meeting the political challenge.

The club was an independent organization, separate from the association. It had its own fees and its own cabinet, and most of its members were young. Only when the club began to face financial difficulties did the young Khalils, the club members, approach Ali for aid. In order to finance the club and, therefore, meet the political challenge, Ali tried to revive the association founded by Abdulkarim in 1951. He learned from Abdulkarim's experience that the failure of the previous association was due to the rivalry for leadership among the seven old branches; hence, his idea of an executive council, composed of seven officials, each representing one branch. The council, as Ali planned it, did not work. Three of the old branches refused to co-operate on the grounds that the council was a trick designed by the Mahdi branch to establish dominance over the other Khalils. According to Ali, those who refused to co-operate were generally the wealthy who aspired to lead the Khalils. Those who co-operated, on the other hand, were of two kinds: those who were genuinely concerned with the political challenge facing the Khalils of Ghobeire, who generally belonged to the old branches of the family, and those who were merely interested in receiving free medical treatment, particularly the newcomers. (This was a reference to the fact that Ali, as a doctor and head of the association, did not charge the Khalil patients, especially the poor ones who supported him politically.) In June 1970 the club was threatened with imminent bankruptcy, while Ali was still trying to get the Khalils to finance it. What he was achieving was a leading role in the politics of the suburb. The longer the club issue continued, the more influential he became: while he was trying to get the Khalils together he was, at the same time, manoeuvring for political support.

4. Another Shi'a family association operating in Ghobeire was the Hashimite association, which had an entirely different organization from that of the Khalils. Established in 1950 by Abu Muhsin al-Musawi, originally from the village of Nabi Shit (district of Baalbek), the Hashimite association included all those

families living in Ghobeire who traced descent to Ali bin Abi Talib, a prominent Hashimite from the Quraysh. These families, known locally as *asyad* (plural of *sayyid*: descendant of imam) claimed descent from Ali through Zain al-Abidin, the son of Husain and grandson of Ali. Husain was the only survivor of the battle of Karbala in Iraq, where Husain's troops lost to those of Yazid in 680. The Hashimite association included many families who had settled in Ghobeire.[3] Being *asyad*, they had a special religious status in Shi'a communities: they personified the continuity of the Imamate. According to Shi'as, the imam is not simply a leader in prayer as he is among the Sunni Muslims, but an interpreter of the word of God, an objective manifestation of the continuity of the line of Ali in whose hands the Caliphate (Islamic government) must rest.

True to its Islamic tradition, the Hashimite association did not 'elect' a cabinet; it designated a secretary. Once a *sayyid* demonstrated his capacity for leadership, he was accepted as the head of the association by sounding out individual opinion, a process referred to as *shura*. To be exact, the association had no head, but a secretary who, with the assistance of an appointed representative from each family, composed the executive board. Like other family associations, the Hashimites' had a written constitution which aimed to unite the *asyad* into one bloc, educate the intelligent, and aid the needy and the sick. Since 1950 the association had only accomplished two things: it gave LL50 to a Murtada *sayyid* who broke his leg in an accident and it erected a Triumphal Arch for King Husain of Jordan (who is a Hashimite) when he visited Lebanon in 1965. Perhaps the money spent on the arch was defrayed by the LL5,000 which King Husain had granted in aid to the association.

According to its founder, Abu Muhsin al-Musawi, the Hashimite association had failed to achieve the main aim for which it was set up, namely, to unite the *asyad* of Ghobeire.

Al-Musawi explained this failure by the 'rivalry for leadership among the *asyad*'. The *asyad* of the suburb, who counted about 83 households, were as divided as the communities from which they originally came. They shared neither the same community background, nor the same political interest, nor even the same genealogy. They were Hashimites by myth, but Musawis, Amins, Murtadas, and so on, by genealogy.

It is difficult here to separate myth from genealogy; but the fact remains that being a Musawi is one thing, but being a Musawi who belongs originally to the Hashimite house (in the distant past) is something else, at least politically. The former is traceable kinship; the latter is an inherited religious title. So intense was the rivalry for leadership between the *asyad* in the municipal elections of 1963 that they were unable to nominate a candidate of their own. Instead, they agreed to support a non-Hashimite. Nevertheless, Abu Muhsin was still trying to unite the *asyad* families in the Hashimite association. When some of the Hashimites began to suspect his leadership, accusing him of using the association as an instrument to further his own personal influence, Abu Muhsin resigned as secretary and began to spread the word that Abdulra'uf al-Amin, an employee in the Ministry of Social Works, was qualified for the office. Few people took this gesture seriously, since it was known in the suburb, at least among the *asyad*, that al-Amin was but the shadow of Abu Muhsin.

5. The last two Shi'a associations which were operating in Ghobeire in 1970 were those of the Rmayti and the Baylun families. They are taken together because the founding of the first was related to that of the second. Both families came originally from the village of Mjadil in the district of Tyre and began to settle in the suburb during the 1950s and 1960s. In the village of their origin, the Rmaytis, who were some 80% of the village population, had a traditional monopoly of the leading positions.

The Bayluns, on the other hand, who composed about 20% of the village, were a sort of pressure group switching support from one Rmayti faction to another, depending on their interests.

In 1955 Muhammad Sa'id Rmayti, an employee in the Ministry of Agriculture in Tyre, came to Ghobeire and invited every adult Rmayti to take part in a general meeting of the family. Though scattered all over the suburb, the Rmaytis, who counted about 17 nuclear families, all attended. At the meeting, Muhammad Sa'id disclosed the founding of a family association and asked those who attended to become members by paying a fee of LL1 a month. He announced that the money would be spent on the construction of a new mosque in Mjadil. 'It is shameful', he said, 'that our village, lacking a good mosque, looks like a Christian rather than a Muslim village.'

Immediately the question of who should collect the fees became a political issue. Finally, it was decided that Ni'mi, Ali and Mahmud, the better-known among the Rmaytis of the suburb, should be authorized to do so. After two years nobody knew who had paid how much or to whom. All knew, however, that a tall minaret had been constructed over the old mosque in Mjadil, under the supervision of Muhammad Sa'id, and that he had begun to build a new house for himself. The three better-known Rmaytis from Ghobeire took issue with Muhammad Sa'id, accusing him of having used the association's money to build a house and threatening to take legal proceedings against him. The case never reached the courts; instead, Muhammad Sa'id returned to them part of the money they had collected and resigned his position in the association. In order to return the money to the original donors, Ni'mi, Ali and Mahmud decided to appoint themselves as the new cabinet of the association, as head, secretary and treasurer respectively. A long time passed, but the money was not redistributed. Moreover, the Rmaytis had not taken a united stand in relation to any issue, even though they retained the cabinet of the association.

Only two months after the Rmaytis formed their association, the Bayluns formed one of their own, under the leadership of Husain Baylun, a shopkeeper. Although similar in some ways to other associations (like them, it claimed to provide education for the poor and aid for the sick and needy, and to unite the family), the Bayluns' differed in its method of organization. Husain, a semi-literate but shrewd manipulator, never bothered to approach the Bayluns collectively. He neither held public meetings nor collected membership fees. Yet he had in his possession a licensed association charter carrying three signatures, his own and two others from the Bayluns. 'To call for a general, collective meeting', he said, 'stirs up jealousies,' adding, 'The Bayluns, after all, are not numerous. I see most of them every day. We talk about the affairs of the association.'

It was here, in the lack of meetings and clear membership, that Husain's reputed influence lay. By holding no meetings and enlisting no members, he had made the association entirely his, dependent on his initiative and effort. When his leadership of the association was verbally challenged by another Baylun, he responded, 'Let him set up another association and become its head.' By holding no public meetings, Husain was able to silence opposition within the family and, at the same time, to keep the size of the association secret. The first tactic earned him the title of unchallenged spokesman of the Bayluns in Ghobeire (he was referred to as an 'election key'); the second earned him a seat in the municipal cabinet. People were so uninformed about the size of the Baylun family that, of those who claimed to know the suburb well, none estimated them to be fewer than 30 nuclear families while, in fact, they counted only 11. Those who made the estimate tried to justify it by saying that the Bayluns had a family association. It appears as if having an association is, in itself, indicative of large family size.

Husain's unchallenged leadership of the Bayluns did not rest entirely on tactical skills, however. He coupled these with tangible commitments. Every Baylun was entitled to a loan from the association, repayable to Husain as interest-free credit, provided that the loan did not exceed LL100. The capital he used for his purpose amounted to LL1,000. It was granted to the association as 'aid' during the parliamentary elections of 1962 by a prominent politician. To many Bayluns, of whom five were vegetable pedlars, this was a significant commitment which provided them with a workable capital. With a capital of LL100, a vegetable pedlar in 1970 could make a profit of LL15–25 a day, thus enabling him to cover his daily expenses and part of his loan.

The rise of family associations must be linked to the changing family structures as these communities grew into suburbs. Before Chiyah and Ghobeire began to develop into suburbs they had a number of leading family groups, each organized around a *bait ma'ruf* (prominent 'house'), an extended family whose pre-eminence in community affairs has been established for at least three generations. The pre-eminence of the *bait ma'ruf*, which is derived from the control of wealth and people, is often expressed in cultural idiom: long genealogies, large families, and a history of migration and settlement. A prominent family confers status on all its relatives, however inconspicuous they may be. Families without a *bait ma'ruf* are classified accordingly as low-status families. The Khalil family had been considered of high status because each of its seven branches, mentioned earlier, was headed by a *bait ma'ruf*. Yet the Khalils were hardly distinguishable from most Ghobeire people. The *bait ma'ruf*, which often leads the family in community affairs, acquires leadership by having socioeconomic assets, i.e. the control of wealth and people. Whoever acquires these assets earns a leading position in the community.

The fact that leadership rests on socioeconomic assets (control of wealth and people) expressed in the cultural idiom (long genealogies, large families, etc) has an important bearing upon the proliferation of family groups into smaller segments. It means that family groups tend to split into smaller segments (often of the lineage order) wherever these segments are organized around new leadership, or new prominent 'houses'. Mobility towards prominent 'houses' carries with it, therefore, a relatively high degree of genealogical segmentation (the splitting off of a line from the main family); this may take place at the primary, secondary or tertiary level depending upon the lineage concerned. In the Ghusn genealogy (Fig. 11), the Ghusns proper split off at the primary level, tracing descent directly to Tannus; the Rishas at the secondary level, tracing descent to Tannus through Risha; and the Khourys and the Dahuds at the tertiary level, tracing descent to Tannus through Abdullah and Jabbour. The tertiary level at which segments are believed to proliferate in other parts of the Middle East (Peters 1967) does not hold true in the suburbs, since within the (Ghusn) genealogy lineages proliferate at three different levels: primary, secondary and tertiary.

Proliferation of lineages is subject to the rise of new leadership, caused either by social mobility or by the dispersal of family groups through migration. This suggests that there is no definite limit at which segments actually split off genealogically. They may split off at the primary, secondary or tertiary descending generations. It also means that there is no definite limit at which segments of comparable structure but of different size can unite. In this sense, family groups which are larger than the nuclear and extended types become historical facts, subject to a great deal of fluctuation. Like empires, family groups expand and shrink depending upon the ambition and power of individual leaders.

What facilitates the expansion and shrinkage of family groups is the fact that links between them are at times recognized to be so fluid that they allow individual segments to shift descent from one line to another without losing their identity. Often, if not always, these shifts are marked by a change of interest or of political loyalty. By claiming to be 'cousins' of the Ghusns, the Ni'mahs, the Zakkurs and the Khallufs gained a wider range of manoeuvrability in local politics. If they allied themselves with the Ghusns, these families would be able to justify their alliance by the 'cousinship' that they claimed to share. Shifts of descent and alliances of this kind are not carried out by family groups as a body, but by individuals, each pursuing his own interests. This is why some Rishas, who allied themselves with the Ghusns, changed their family names to Ghusn when the latter became prominent in the area. While becoming prominent, a man simultaneously enlarges his family.

Large families do not necessarily produce prominent men; the definition of a family group, lineage or clan, in terms of a fixed set of generations that reaches to a fixed ancestor, must be qualified. Obviously, this definition tends to reflect the micro-methods used by anthropologists to record their data rather than the way family groups actually behave. The analysis of relatively small localized family groups, whose members engage in intensive interaction, is apt to yield well-defined lines of descent. Whether descent itself is exact, or is made so as a result of intensive interaction, is difficult to demonstrate because it requires the charting of descent lines of the same family over a number of generations. As regards small localized family groups, the definition of lineage by criteria of descent (a fixed set of generations) coincides with the definition of group by sociometric (interaction) criteria (Homans 1951: 82–4). In the suburbs family size determined by genealogical depth is a measure of the prominence of family leaders. Lineages cannot be defined by descent lines alone: exact genealogies, which are considered to be characteristic of lineages, are merely the cultural expression of corporate actions manipulated by leaders.

This brief account of family organization and proliferation seems necessary for an understanding of the family associations in Chiyah and Ghobeire. The founding of such associations depended upon two conditions: competitive leadership and genealogical ambiguity. These phenomena became more widespread in the suburbs in the early 1950s as a result of the economic boom and the social and spatial (migration) mobility accruing therefrom. The way to translate prosperity into status is to challenge the leader of one's own family. This challenge may take several forms: refusing to support the leader in times of conflict, criticizing him in public, carrying on social transactions on the basis of strict reciprocity, or trying to become leader. In becoming leader, a man first seeks the support of his kin, which he can accomplish either by gradually eliminating the already established leadership (if the family has any) or by splitting himself off from the main family group. When a potential leader splits off from the main family, he takes with him his supporters, who often happen to be his close relatives; thus he forms a separate lineage, branch, segment, and so on. If this process continues for two or three generations, the political cleavage within the family results in genealogical segmentation. Here again, lack of social interaction, caused by political disagreements, expresses itself culturally in genealogical proliferation. Family groups with many prosperous individuals would be expected therefore to be politically more splintered (in the sense of having multi-leadership) and genealogically more proliferated. This was indeed the case of the Khalils of Ghobeire and the Ghusns of Chiyah.

The stability of resources in Chiyah and Ghobeire before these villages became suburbs, and the limited mobility, social or spatial, that resulted from this stability, contributed to steady family leadership and thus slow proliferation. On the other hand, relative prosperity and high mobility (including migration), which came while Chiyah and Ghobeire were changing into suburbs, gave rise to intense competition for family leadership and, thereafter, increasing genealogical proliferation. Increasing proliferation, caused either by mobility or by migration, creates genealogical ambiguities, not so much regarding the distant origin of the family as the actual linkages that tie the living groups together (the Ghusns are a case in point).

In the face of multi-leadership within the family coupled with genealogical uncertainties, family associations present themselves as logical outlets for whoever seeks to control the family he belongs to. By establishing a formally recognized association, the founder avoids the intricate question of who is related to whom and in what manner. He simply accepts the given situation—whoever carries the family name or shares in its mythical origin becomes eligible for membership regardless of his place of residence, place of birth or the exact position he occupies on a genealogical map.

In other words, the leader creates an anti-lineage organization whose membership is voluntary. And by creating an anti-lineage organization that rests on the myth of family origin, the founder/leader earns the initiative to act on a broader base than the small, localized segments. The range within which he can manoeuvre for support becomes as wide as he wants it to be. For example, Kadhim al-Khalil, wanting to play a role in national politics, founded an association with nation-wide links that could be traced, presumably, to Abraham. By contrast, Ali al-Khalil, who wanted to play an active role in the local politics of Ghobeire, confined membership to those who carried the family name and lived in the suburb, regardless of whether they were old or new settlers. His interest was regional, whereas Kadhim's was national. Like Ali al-Khalil, Husain Baylun, whose aim was to be the spokesman of the Bayluns in Ghobeire, founded an association there; but, unlike Ali, he thought that in order to remain the unchallenged leader of the Bayluns he had to avoid recruiting members or holding public meetings. In his view, recruiting members and holding meetings would raise suspicion, invite competition and expose the weakness of the association—in other words, how small it was.

Of all the associations, active or inactive, founded in the suburbs since 1950, two, the Bayluns' and the Khalils', seemed to be still active in 1970, which was in itself a measure of success. The other two associations, the Hashimites' and the Rmaytis', though they had a nominal cabinet, had not made any decisions for a long time, which suggests that they were no longer active and were almost certainly sinking into oblivion—a common fate of family associations. The question that logically poses itself here is, why do family associations cease to exist almost as soon as they are founded?

Founding an association 'to unite the family' does not, by itself, achieve unity. A family association provides the founder/leader with a platform, free from strict lineage ties, to manoeuvre for support. Once an association is founded, it is then the job of the leader to gather support. Likewise, the fact that associations enable leaders to ignore the barring effects of strict lineage ties does not eliminate lineage loyalties; it simply suspends them for a while. As demonstrated in the case of the Hashimite, Khalil, Ghusn and Rmayti family associations, strong loyalty to individual lineages militates against family unity.

Besides, to be a founder is to claim leadership, not necessarily to lead. So wary are other potential leaders of the political ambitions of the founder that they tend to oppose him at every public meeting. The timing of such meetings is also significant. General meetings are usually called for just before local or national elections, which makes members suspicious of the founder's political intentions. After elections the association is suspended, if not entirely forgotten, until the next elections. Even in the case of the active associations of the Bayluns and the

Khalils, the political intentions of the founders were well known—except that Husain, the president of the first association, justified his political ambitions by the credit system he had made available, and Ali, the president of the second association, by continuous medical aid. Regarding the latter association, the prosperous Khalils, who had no need of free medical treatment, still continue to challenge Ali's leadership.

Sooner or later, Ali will realize that to head a family association does not influence his popularity negatively or positively. Likewise, Husain's association might very well be forgotten once his credit system becomes unnecessary. Political leadership is based on the continuous provision of services, not on prestige positions, such as the leadership of a family association. What family associations do, in fact, is initially to 'feature' (to borrow a word from archaeology) a potential leader. It is worth stressing the word 'initially', for herein lies the sociological significance of family associations, as well as the reasons for their transient, non-enduring character. As an anti-lineage organization, based on genealogical mythologies that can be stretched lineally, and therefore horizontally, as far as the founder wants, a family association simply lays down the initial foundations, the frame of reference, for political action. Whether or not the founder stands up to the test of leadership is largely determined by his personal ability afterwards. In either case, whether the leader succeeds or fails, the association loses the initial function for which it was set up. Accordingly, it may be suspended or forgotten, or it may turn into a social club, as did the Bustani family association soon after it was founded towards the turn of the century.

Family associations are anti-group organizations where groups (in this case lineages) dwarf individual mobility. The non-lasting relationships that they create act as a lubricant that helps to transfer a man from one status to another, either from an ordinary family member to a spokesman, or from a leader of a branch to a family leader, and then to a national leader. Once the transfer from one status to another is achieved, the association, constituted of equals, loses its function and is accordingly forgotten. Hence, its manipulative character.

6
Emirs and *Ulama*: Alliances and Collective Action

The game is for the first to dominate his equals, thus becoming a *taiyar*, a *dama* or an imam. The single measure of differentiation in Arab culture is dominance, or power. It is not surprising that Ibn Khaldun adopted the power-based model of the *asabiya-mulk* syndrome to analyse the essentials of Arab society. Ibn Khaldun's concepts of *mulk* and *umran* combine urban and state institutions. His concept of *asabiya*, which connotes internal solidarity based on tribal and/or religious affiliation, implies social corporation lacking private ownership, the accumulation of wealth or formal hierarchical structures. These constitute the *mulk* stage of a collectivity that transforms itself from a nomadic status to a ruling urban elite. This stage, believes Ibn Khaldun, marks the beginning of decline. In other words, a solidarity maintained by egalitarian ethics is doomed when it is transformed into a hierarchically arranged structure—the state. Metaphorically, a human group is strong in a backgammon-like environment and weak in a chess-like situation.

It is power that sets the elite, or upper classes, apart from the others. Consider the nomenclature by which the upper classes are known in Arabic: the possessors of influence, the possessors of popularity, men of contacts, the prominent 'houses', the fronts,

the eyes, the faces and the heads of the community.[1] Note that
these latter terms refer to the upper parts of the body. The rich in
Arab society who command no power pay tribute in public to the
poor who are strong. In the Gulf countries the urban, non-tribal
rich show deference to all the ruling families, whether rich or
poor.

In economic terms, three classes can be distinguished: the poor
or needy (*muhtajun*), the self-sufficient (*masturun*) and the affluent
(*maysurun*). These are distinguished by their way of life, which is
basically determined by economic capacity (Khuri 1969; 1975:
78–90). Even the terms by which these classes are known (needy,
self-sufficient and affluent) reflect an economic bias. Within
these classes, mobility can be achieved within a person's lifetime
by increasing one's income and upgrading the way of life
associated with it. But moving up to a still higher status—the
notables, or *zu'ama* class, who command power and authority—
may take several generations. It is only with time that wealth can
be translated into social power. The *usul* tribes in the Arab Gulf,
who occupy high status, dominate the client tribes. You become
usul because you dominate.

If you have power you are an emir; if you do not you are the
'made weak' (*mustad'af*)—of course, made so by the emir himself.
The word 'emir' is derived from the verbal root *amara*, which
means to order or instruct. Much like emir, many an Arabic word
signifying leadership likewise implies acts of verbal imperatives:
the word *za'im* (political leader) comes from *za'ama*, meaning to
assume; and *qa'id* (leader) comes from *qala*, meaning to say. It is not
surprising that leaders are also known as 'the possessors of
eloquence' (*ahl mantiq*). Emirs give orders but do not receive them,
even concerning such an insignificant matter as the departure
time of a train or a flight. The escort of an Arab emir observed,
while in Europe:

You simply say nothing! You sit down burning inside, afraid you may miss the train or the plane, and the emir takes no notice of anything around him. All are ready to move, but the emir takes his time. If he misses the train that would be the will of God.

Social authority is not built into a graded structure of offices, but rather into a rigidly stratified system of ritualistic communication: the higher the rank, the more rigid the communication system. It is a ritualized system in which social distance is inflexible.

The porcelain-looking faces of rulers and princes in the Arab Gulf are meant to keep a distance. Laughing, joking and touch all establish intimacy and narrow social distance and are therefore shunned at public, formal meetings. The presence of the emir is a solemn occasion; one silently listens all the time and talks only if asked to. While talking to an emir , pleading for God's mercy by the use of phrases such as *in sha'a allah* (if God so wishes), *ma sha'a allah* (whatever God wishes) and *al-hamdu li-allah* (thanks to God) is highly desirable, but swearing repeatedly by God's name is abhorred. (The Nejdi Arabs often swear by their sisters; their 'war cry' always refers to sisters—sisters and daughters represent men's honour.)

While talking to an emir or a *za'im*, one should avoid phrases implying secrecy or confidentiality, such as: 'between you and me', 'strictly confidentially between us' and 'I'm saying this for the first time.' These phrases imply equality between interactors, and in the presence of the emir nobody is equal to him. This is perhaps the reason that emirs and *za'ims* do not meet other emirs publicly at large gatherings, each having built around himself his own audience and retinue—councils (tents) duplicating themselves horizontally on a 'flat' plane. Emirs do not visit; they are visited. Their 'houses are open'.

Emirs dominate their councils through dyadic relationships

rotating around themselves, the axes. It is not that they care to follow every single movement around them, but people around them do not make 'movements' without trying first to catch their attention. Many a speaker stops talking as soon as the emir moves his eyes sideways to listen to somebody else. Seated strategically in the centre of the back seat facing the entrance door of his council, the emir handles each and all spontaneously and simultaneously.

In the emir's council, the seating order is the 'barometer' of status. The higher in rank are seated serially closer to the emir on his right side; the left is spiritually 'polluted' (*najis*), good only for toilet-cleaning. Lower ranks are seated on the left side. Should there be no one of any consequence in the council, the seats on the emir's immediate right and left remain empty, sometimes filled with telephone lines.

A man wanting to know his 'worth' should observe the position of the seat to which he is ushered. To be seated close to the emir reflects the person's status and the emir's interest. No one enters the council of the emir without previous arrangement; the idea that an emir has his 'council' open for twenty-four hours to receive guests haphazardly is classic Arabian fiction. This may happen at times among nomads living in the open, barren desert, but not in cities. Visiting the emir is a well-structured event: who, why and for what purpose have to be spelled out in advance. In the Arab Gulf, people of means and status greet the emir by mutually rubbing noses or shoulders; others by bowing to hold his knee or foot. Kissing rather than rubbing the emir's nose is a sign of subservience to his will.

However, Arab society is not class-marked, where social standings are clearly differentiated. A person's social value is directly linked to the purpose of his visit. Visiting the emir to swear allegiance or to discuss issues and negotiate deals takes priority over requests appealing for financial aid: building houses, mending fences, paying bridewealth or going abroad for education. Those who appeal for financial aid, called *shirha* in Saudi Arabia, write their requests on a piece of paper and rush to kneel before the emir, slipping their body gently between his legs (a sexual position) while placing the written request in his lap. The emir takes the note in his hand and promises aid in the name of God, the Most Generous. The mere act of being admitted to the emir's council means that the request will be granted.

Close associates of the emir rarely, if ever, visit him openly in the council where he receives guests and visitors. They meet privately at home or in the office. In the presence of the emir, people sit with their legs parallel to each other, not crossed. The emir looks people in the eye; when he stares at his visitors, they are expected to shift their eyes sideways to the floor. Staring back at the emir is an act of defiance.

The first form of interaction people encounter centres around honorific and courtesy titles, and here people are roughly divided into emirs and commoners. In the Gulf, emirs wear black or white robes (*mashlah*), striped on two sides, with the right flank flowing over the body and the left one cast over the shoulder and often carried in the hand. The best kind of *mashlah*, costing around 100,000 Saudi riyals, is made of *mir'iz* hair, which is a very rare goat species. Non-emirs do not use this form of dress.

The distinction in headdress is made between emirs and commoners, on the one hand, and the *ulama* of religion, on the other. Only the first category wear the *iqal* (the rope-like ribbon) over the headcloth (*kufiya* or *ghitra*). The Ghutghut shaikhs of Nejd (Saudi Arabia), who are strict observers of religious laws, occupy the highest position among the *ulama*. They are the descendants of those who fought side by side with King Abdulaziz to unite the kingdom in the early part of this century. Some social and regional variations can be observed in the colour of the headdress. Whereas the people of Nejd may wear coloured *kufiyas*, the

Hijazis wear white ones. Only King Abdulaziz and King Faisal wore striped *iqals*. The word *iqal* means harness; apparently the *ulama*, who are 'harnessed' by religious knowledge, need not be harnessed by ribbons, striped or unstriped.

All emirs are addressed by the title 'emir' preceding their first names: Emir Fahd, Emir Muhammad, and so on. An emir from the Al-Saud is addressed as *sumuw al-amir* (Prince Highness), and those who are sons of kings are addressed as *sahib al-sumuw al-malaki* (Lord Royal Highness). The Al-Saud themselves also observe these forms of address even when interacting among themselves. Formality governs their day-to-day interaction; the younger among them address the older as *sidi* (Lord or Master).

Emirs are also addressed in direct speech as *ya tawil al-umr* (ye. . .of long life). The phrase *tal umrak* (May your life be prolonged) is a pause in speech which can be used by anyone. However, when an emir uses the phrase *tal umrak*, this indicates closeness and familiarity, signifying favourable relationships. Commoners inquire about the emir's health as a person; the emir responds by inquiring about the commoner's family.

Even with their intimate associates, whom they meet in private, emirs keep their distance. They never allow any form of personal interaction. At private meetings, they smile, laugh and tease people they like, but theirs is a one-way traffic. They tease you, you don't tease them. You don't laugh, you laugh with them. It is gratifying to be teased by an emir. If he likes you very much, he calls you 'brother'; otherwise he uses your first name without a title.

Emirs talk about various subjects—business, philosophy, religious traditions, oil prices, international politics, Israel, falconry, hunting, horses, desert life, camel racing, boats, and so on—sometimes knowledgeably and sometimes less so. In either case, the audience listen, nod their heads in agreement and rarely, if ever, interrupt to correct the emir. As one associate commented,

'Keeping the emir's company is constraining, a form of imprisonment. You can never be yourself. You are always treated as a subordinate!'

Emirs are so sensitive about status that they often break off relations with associates who occupy high posts in government and subsequently earn high honorific titles, sometimes higher than those of the emirs themselves. Many a technocrat, upon becoming a member of a cabinet or a political leader of some consequence, has lost his credibility among the tribal emirs. Emirs do not like to see associates assuming a higher status than themselves. 'There is no "Your Highness" in the council of the emir other than the emir himself,' commented another associate.

Emirs dominate their councils and courts to such an extent that the moment they leave, the 'party' they have created evaporates. The speed with which the crowd around them disappear with the emirs' departure makes the matter even more dramatic, since the decision to terminate the party is often taken abruptly without previous notice. When they decide to move, everybody moves. Minutes before their departure from a place, it is packed with well-wishers; minutes afterwards, it begs solitude—like a desert storm that blows over as soon as it arises.

The emir's trust is assumed and cannot be taken for granted. It is an ambivalent situation in which a person can easily get lost. The emir calls you 'brother', invites you home, allows his *haram* (wife) to meet you unveiled, accepts your invitations, plays poker or backgammon with you, borrows money from you and never bothers to return it, teases you, drinks with you, even shares 'nightlife' with you; but he still expects you to open the car door for him, hand him a glass of water or whisky, and be ready to respond to his requests at whatever hour of the day. The first group of interactions imply equality and respect of status; the second clearly imply subordination.

Emirs often manipulate time to enforce a situation of

subordination. Failing to return phone calls, ignoring appointments, delaying meetings, letting a visitor wait for hours or even days before acknowledging his presence or request— these are meant to subordinate statuses, thus pushing the interactor into an inferior position.

Collective Action through Alliances

Using data mainly from the Gulf, the foregoing discussion has attempted to show that in the absence of a clearly laid down hierarchic structure, dominance (the art of subordinating others) is achieved through a rigidly stratified system of communication. The structure is one of a rimless wheel built into a series of dyadic relationships linking followers—called *khwaiyan* in Saudi Arabia, which is a diminutive form of brother (*akh*)—into the emir or imam, the locus of interaction. While retaining authority within his own circle, an emir or imam could simultaneously be a chequer in somebody else's circle or *khanat* of a higher order (Fig. 12).

A, B and C, the emirs, control their respective followers by providing a variety of services and acting as mediators. A is linked to the (a)s, B to the (b)s and C to the (c)s through different sorts of allegiance built into family, fealty or feudal ties. But A, B and C are also linked to each other through a chain of alliances created by mutual interests. It is a 'constellation' rather than a pyramidal structure. I use the word 'constellation' metaphorically to indicate: the absence of hierarchically arranged roles; the freedom with which individual groups revolving around emirs, imams or leaders manage their affairs independently from other groups; and the fluidity of alliances between imams and emirs. It is a game of backgammon, moving the stones across the board by building *khanats* that generate *taiyars*.

My field research on political leadership in the suburbs of Beirut (Khuri 1975: chs. 6 & 7), the Sunni and Shi'a *ulama* (Khuri

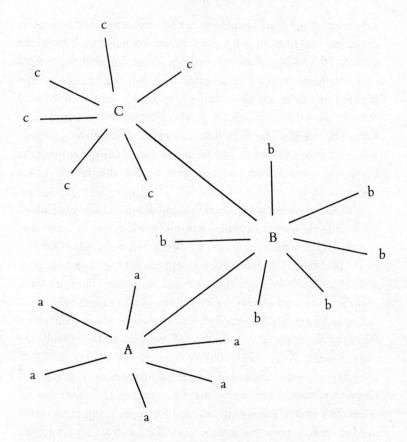

Figure 12: 'Constellation' Form of Organization

1987) and the organization of Alawi and Druze religious shaikhs (Khuri 1988: ch. 16) all clearly demonstrate the constellation-like principle of organization in Arab culture. The Alawi religious organization is based on individual dyads permeating the whole community; it is a series of master-novice relationships that cut across tribal factions. The master, called *amm*, sees to it that the novices' religious obligations are fulfilled from birth to death.

Likewise, among the Druzes, lesser shaikhs are linked to higher, more learned ones in religious fellowships that reach from the bottom (the village shaikhs) to the top few (by 1989 there were three of them) who are distinguished by wearing the cylindrical turban. This is much like small-group leaders in the suburbs of Beirut, known as 'election keys', who graft themselves onto more influential national leaders, the *zu'ama* class, thus forming nation-wide coalitions that often cut across sects and regions. Among the *ulama*, the constellation may reach far beyond the boundary of a region or state.

The 42 Sunni *ulama* I studied in some depth in Lebanon (Khuri 1987: 291–312) were organized in 'network constellations' that cut across the formal structure of *shari'a* courts. Whether central or peripheral, individual courts operated with a large degree of autonomy and with no hierarchical structure binding them together into a single authority system. Appeal cases were only voluntarily referred to higher learned *ulama* for consultation. Some of those *ulama* even operated independently outside the court system (Khuri 1987: 300).

However, this non-pyramidal structure, or segmental autonomy, should not be construed as meaning that there was no concerted action among the *ulama*. Instead of being built into a graded authority system with lower offices hierarchically linked to higher offices, unity of action was built into a complex system of networks with the less learned *ulama* linked to the more learned. Drawn on the basis of, first, the power to employ and, second, religious consultation and appeal, these networks operated at the local, national or international level, sometimes involving links with the outer Islamic world.

The bureaucratic arrangement of *shari'a* courts does not reflect the centrality of interaction in the syndrome of networks that bind the *ulama* together inside or outside the same political entity. It is a fluid system that allows a jurist to hold a central position in a specific network while occupying a peripheral post in the bureaucratic structure of the *shari'a* courts, and vice versa. Some *ulama*, after retirement, continue to deliberate on legal controversies referred to them sometimes by the court itself, which necessarily undermines the authority of the *shari'a* office. Some have been officiating on legal matters reaching much beyond the boundaries of the individual state—a phenomenon that reflects on the quality of state sovereignty as well as on the structure of the Islamic *umma*. When Ayatollah Khumaini ordered the death of Salman Rushdie[2] in 1989, he was acting in his capacity as a judge in the Islamic *umma* whose authority reached far beyond the immediate boundaries of a single sovereign state. The British government took the *fatwa* as an affront to its sovereignty. It was a matter of state versus *umma*, or metaphorically, chess versus backgammon—the latter being styled after the universe, where the whole world is considered an arena for action.

7
Endogamy: A Recipe for Autocratic Rule

I have always wondered why Arabs prefer to marry their cousins, to be visited by others rather than to visit, and to interact with the world as if it is made up of brothers and sisters or uncles and aunts; why they take pride in long genealogies, boast about family origin, abhor hierarchies and admire brotherhoods, rebel against states and worship the *umma* (community). The answer lies in the fact that imams and emirs, the 'firsts', come from within the group, the solidarity composed of equals. It is an endogamous culture. In other words, as people move up the social scale, they turn their relationships inwards rather than outwards as an expression of achievement, upward mobility and high status. Endogamy is a much-admired way of life.

The ethnographic literature on Arab culture shows that the rate of in-marriage among high-status people is far higher than among commoners. The *usul* (those who are in-bred) marry within their own kind, whereas the commoners follow a haphazard marriage pattern. Endogamous behaviour is a general process; it is practised in marriage, visits, neighbourhood organizations, work, friendship groups, associations and court organization. In the Gulf countries, members of the ruling families visit each other but do not visit outsiders; the lower in rank among them visit the higher in rank. They cluster in specific sections of the city. They employ and work for each other, and do not seek employment outside. They have their own sports clubs and family courts presided over by the head of state.

Long genealogies are an expression of power, the exploits of the strong. The 'weak' who talk about family exploits and quote long genealogies are ridiculed. Genealogical depth, the privilege of the strong, implies achievement and historical notability; the longer the genealogy, the wider the range of relatives. It is in the interests of a leader to seek deeper genealogies and thus expand his potential supporters, inviting more people to become relatives. Through this process of expansion, coupled with a series of endogamous practices, an *asabiya* (solidarity) is formed. Endogamous practices generate *asabiya* formulations and the internal cohesion of groups. By controlling marriages, visits, neighbourhoods, friendships, associations, courts and clubs, a leader controls the group. Endogamous practices are the mechanisms through which an *asabiya* (a *khanat*) is formed.

Once formed, *asabiyat* (solidarities) are grafted onto bigger and higher ones, thus forming a monolithic structure through a chain of alliances. (Interestingly, political action and architectural plans can be described in almost the same words.) Unlike allegiances within a solidarity, which may persist for a long time, alliances between solidarities change with political circumstances. The first are built on lasting commitments—family obligations, fealty ties, common ownership of property, and so on; the second are based on shifting immediate interests. How these solidarities actually operate in different contexts will be demonstrated in the following discussion on: (1) city ecology in Beirut before and during the ongoing Lebanese war; and (2) tribalism and state structures in the Gulf. These two illustrations have been chosen to show how endogamous behaviour operates in entirely unrelated spheres of action. Needless to say, the theme can be generalized to other domains as well.

City Ecology

In my previous work on urbanization in Beirut just before the war (Khuri 1975), the literature on urban social ecology had misled me into believing that cities have inner areas ringed by stratified residential belts (working-class houses, the homes of the middle classes and the commuter zone) and surrounded by suburbs, and that all of these zones, rings and belts make up the totality of the city. This view is referred to in the literature on urbanism as 'the Chicago School', following Wirth, Park, McKenzie and Burgess who worked in and on Chicago. Burgess (1938: 218), for example, divided Chicago into five 'concentric circles' encompassing the entire city limits.

My data on the suburbs of Beirut did not conform to this model of analysis, as evidenced by the generality and independence of the socioeconomic organization of individual suburbs. Unlike Western suburbia, the Beirut suburbs lack specialization and tend to develop multifunctional services in the sense that jobs, services, recreational centres, schools, clubs, welfare societies, places of worship, cultural activities, banks and hospitals are all centred in individual suburbs. Thus a person may find all the necessary daily services within a radius of some 200 metres. Because of this generality and independence some 91% of the labour force in my work (1975: 214) were found residing within the suburb's limits; the rest (9%) commuted to different parts of the neighbouring areas for work.

What is called the city-centre, al-Burj, in Beirut did not strictly speaking serve the urban communities in the city. The city-centre was simply an extension of the port and it operated as a terminus for traffic coming from the countryside. Were it not for the heavily centralized bureaucracy in the country, which had led to the concentration of services and facilities in the capital (Beirut), the Burj area would have been far less active than it actually was. In other words, the city-centre was a *suq* (market-place) that served the whole nation and not simply an organic part of the city structure *par excellence*; it happened to be in Beirut, close to the port. In fact, many cities in the Middle East like Fez, Aleppo, San'a, Damascus, and so on, had (and many continue to have) weekly *suqs* located outside the city limits. Literally speaking, they have no 'downtowns' or city-centres.

The image of Beirut as a single organism, where the parts constitute an integrated whole, does not reflect socioeconomic realities. It is better seen as a series of individual 'tents' bound together in a constellation-like form rather than a single, monolithic unit. This same image or model is observed in Abu-Lughod's (1971) work on Cairo, where she refers to the 'tents' as 'sub-cities' that have emerged at different times in the history of Cairo. With some alterations, the same observation holds true of other cities as well. For example, the city of al-Ain in Abu Dhabi today is inhabited by various tribal factions, each clustering in a specific section of town; so was Basra at the onset of the Muslim Arab conquest.

Perhaps nowhere was this image of the city, as made up of a series of 'tents' or semi-independent urban nuclei, illustrated more vividly than during the Lebanese war. Conflict situations sometimes illustrate the pattern or norm better than non-conflict conditions. In a survey carried out in 1980 with the help of graduate students at the Department of Social and Behavioural Sciences of the American University of Beirut, I counted 32 para-political, para-military 'associations' (local militias) that had spread through different sections of the city of Beirut. Built upon a series of social solidarities, these associations had divided the city into mutually exclusive spheres or zones of influence, or what they called 'operation grounds'; the presence of one excluded the others. Even two sides of the same street might each be under the control of a different 'association'.

This is precisely where straight streets laid down according to a geometric design may be an embarrassment; they are difficult to divide socially and then politically and militarily. The twisted streets of Beirut, like other Middle Eastern cities, are a mirror of social agglomerations interwoven by kinship and traditional ties of neighbourliness. In some micro-research on a small neighbourhood in Ras Beirut, I found that buildings are erected on plots subdivided according to inheritance patterns. The social assemblage matters more than the physical design; the urban society is fitted into a social map, not a spatial one. This may explain the virtual absence of public gardens and the disrespect for anything 'public'. (The word *umumi*, meaning public, immediately brings two things to mind: a shared taxi, which is called in Arabic an *umumi* car, and a brothel, which is called an *umumi suq*.)

Although the para-political, para-military associations in Beirut were grafted onto wider political organizations—in 1980 many of them adopted PLO slogans—this did not eliminate the measure of independence they enjoyed in dealing with local affairs within individual neighbourhoods. Indeed, in 1978 when the PLO tried to incorporate these local militias into its military body, it met with resistance and the attempt was consequently withdrawn. With the withdrawal of the PLO from Beirut following the Israeli invasion in 1982, these very militia-solidarities shifted to a pro-Iranian, pro-Syrian position. It appears that these local micro-militias rush to adopt macro-political ideologies just to safeguard their local autonomy and close in upon themselves as unpenetrable solidarities. Through this process of enclosure, they ward off the possibility of being assimilated into impersonal national structures.

It is precisely this double process of 'grafting' and 'enclosure' that works against the rise of free and open party political systems, as well as free and open urban neighbourhoods and, therefore, macro-'horizontal' structures (the public) of any kind. As soon as these free and open macro-movements begin to develop, built-in endogamous solidarities creep in, capture the inner moral authority of the movement, and redirect its orientation inwardly again in order to reinforce the endogamous character of the solidarity itself. Consider, for example, how Wahhabism reinforced the endogamous character of the Al-Saud in Saudi Arabia and how the Ba'th Party reinforced the endogamous character of a sectarian community in Syria (the Alawis) and a 'village' community in Iraq (the Tikritis).

The theme of this chapter is that the city ecology—like many other macro-structures such as political parties, national liberation mass movements and religious movements—is built around a series of endogamous solidarities that graft themselves, through chains of alliances, onto the general body without being assimilated into it. This is why it sometimes seems as if what matters in a conflict situation is not the resolution of the conflict as much as the attainment of the group's social solidarity.

The explanation lies in the ideological insistence on endogamy as a desired way of life, a model of social mobility in Arab culture. 'Endogamy' is used here in a generalized sense to refer to a wide variety of actions, behaviours, beliefs, customs and practices which include, among other things, marriage, visits, class distinctions, group formation, ethnicity, and so on. It is indeed a syndrome of preferences. By understanding the endogamous character of Arab culture, it is then possible to appreciate its various political and organizational characteristics, including the organization of urban life.

It is important to realize, at the outset, that there are no secondary associations, 'lodges' or 'rites of passage' in Arab culture that interfere in the process of socialization other than the family, whether nuclear or extended. As previously mentioned, given the practice of first-cousin marriage, it is possible for two married siblings to constitute a total society. Within this small kinship unit a person is able to fulfil all the necessary cultural requirements of life, focusing on birth, puberty and death.

Life is a process that continues uninterrupted by the stages of biological growth; the category of *shabab* (youth) groups together males between 6 and 60. Just as this explains why many militia organizations train children as young as 6, it also explains the absence of public playgrounds for children, and, for that matter, why Arabs tend to be intelligent rather than innovative. The fitting of children into adult models restricts the imagination and curbs inventiveness.

Believers see life continuing after death, and religion (*al-din*) as organizing people's life here and in the hereafter. Religion in Islam does not stand in opposition to this world (*al-dunya*); this world stands in opposition to the other world (*al-akhirah*), and religion organizes both. In this continuing and uninterrupted process, a person is seen as a link in a chain (*silsila*), and the chain as a single solidarity. It is interesting to note that the concept of solidarity and internal cohesion is often symbolically expressed in words signifying a series of individual elements: *silsila* (chain), *tasalsul* (descent), *sulala* (genealogy), *habl* (rope or cable, as in the Qur'an, 3/103: 'And hold fast, all of you together, to the cable of Allah, and do not separate'), *nasab* (patrilineality; also meaning alliance, *tahaluf*), *hasab* (matrilineal male predecessors; also meaning high social reputation), *takatuf* (shoulder to shoulder) and *ta'adud* (pillar to pillar). No wonder strings of beads have such wide popular appeal in Arab culture; the Arabs call them 'praise' (*sabbaha*) beads, not 'worry' beads, as is often falsely translated into English. In other words, the Arabs praise through beads; they do not worry.

Obviously, the person, as 'link', is believed to be bound to a group, a 'chain', formulated on the basis of genealogy, descent or lineage; a person is therefore distinguished by the solidarity thus formulated. People of high status are known as *usul* or *ansab*, meaning a kinship category with a long, traceable genealogy. Indeed *asil* (in-bred) horses are those whose ancestors are known, and *ta'sil* means inbreeding. Arabs inbreed (*yu'assil*) horses, camels, hawks (for hunting) and dogs, all of which are prestige investments often possessed by people of high status and social notability.

Because of these ideological formulations, endogamy and social enclosure become desirable models of action and behaviour. Endogamous behaviour is an instrument to attain 'enclosure' and, therefore, internal solidarity. The ethnographic record on Arab society strongly supports this conclusion, as evidenced by several factors: the high ratio of intermarriage among the *usul*; the 'one-way traffic' between notables and commoners, where the latter visit the former but not vice versa; the tendency for high-status families to cluster together; and the expression of high status by long genealogical records, i.e. as soon as a person achieves notability through wealth, power or professional practice, he adopts, along with it, a long genealogy of origin. In brief, as people move up the social ladder, they turn inwardly rather than outwardly, thus becoming *khassa* (the private ones) rather than *amma* (commoners). While the West tends to focus on the 'private' life of the elites, such as marriage, divorce, travel, hobbies, and so on, in the Middle East the focus is on the elites' formal and public engagements: visits, projects, meetings and meals. In Arab society, when a commoner meets a notable he greets him with 'peace'. The notable responds by asking about the commoner's wives, homes, children, jobs, work, earnings; but for the notable, these are private matters that he will never divulge in public. The notables are the *khassa*, the privately enclosed solidarity.

Many other customs, concepts and practices in Arab culture, including honour and shame, face (*wajh*), revenge and vengeance, kinship systems and organizations, can be dealt with as instruments of endogamy that turn relations inward rather than outward. However, what concerns us here is the way or ways in which endogamy as an ideological system, a desirable model of action, bears upon urban living. And in this connection, two related fields of action and behaviour must be stressed: first, the image of the city as composed of a series of semi-independent solidarities that are distinguished socially and ethnically, and sometimes politically and economically; and second, the sharp division between private and public domains, with obvious moral preference given to the private. In other words, there is a clear relationship between endogamous forms of action and behaviour, as desirable models, and the constitution of cities as a series of 'tents' or urban nuclei, each corresponding to a particular social solidarity and having the very facilities and services enjoyed by the others. Social solidarity may express itself sometimes in ethnic terms, sometimes in religious and sectarian idiom, and sometimes in kinship, community-based ties; or even in the three arenas of action woven together into a single solidarity, each reinforcing the others.

The stress on endogamous behaviour as a desirable model of action also makes 'the public', however defined, take on a secondary moral value. What matters is 'the private' domain, especially women and the family; everything else—space, streets, traffic, parking, garbage, gardens, schools, states, laws—is of secondary importance. The ease with which public property is 'confiscated' in Beirut, without people raising any objection, supports the point. Private shops fencing off a segment of the street to designate it as their own; flower shops and pedlars occupying the pavement; parking or double parking in any open space; confiscating part of the highway in order to extend a

127

building plot; stealing electricity from municipal cables—all these scenes occur so frequently in Beirut, as in many other Arab cities, that they easily pass unnoticed. Not only do people ignore these misdeeds, but to the actors, they are a source of pride and a measure of dominance—a *taiyar* (free) set of actions.

Tribalism and State Structures in the Arab Gulf

As an expression of endogamy, tribalism signifies a social group and not an ecological one; it is a type of solidarity that can be found in cities, villages and nomadic camps. In Arab society, there are tribal nomads, tribal peasants and tribal urban people. Tribalism is a form of social organization that cuts across ecological conditions. Conversely, there are cases of single tribes, like the Fa'ours of Syria and the Rabi'as of Kuwait and Iraq, who simultaneously contain nomadic, peasant and urban people.

A solidarity is called tribal because it manipulates kinship as an instrument to enforce endogamous practices. In the Gulf, people are classified into tribal (*qabali*) or urban (*madani*) categories depending upon genealogical links. Tribal categories are *ansab*, i.e. those with traceable genealogies. The others have no traceable origin and are often called *bani-khudair*, 'the sons of green'. In the Gulf, they were mostly employed in the pearl-diving industry in the nineteenth century and the early part of the twentieth.

At the national level of political action, all people of tribal origin are grouped under the *qabili* faction, who are recruited into the army, the national guard, the police force and other paramilitary structures. Whereas the *qabili* dominate the power-based state structures, the *madini* dominate the technical ones. The *qabili* faction, headed by the ruling family, acts as if it were a political party cutting across various segments in society through a series of alliances with tribal solidarities. Alliances with other tribal solidarities are sustained by out-marriages whereby men of the ruling families marry women of client tribes.

In this sense, one has to distinguish between tribal states and tribally controlled states. Strictly speaking, there are no tribal states in Arab society today. A 'tribe' in tribal society is a complete, self-sufficient, autonomous system that derives its authority from within. In tribally controlled states, on the other hand, a 'tribe' (*qabili*) is a part society, a political faction that competes for power within state structures. The tribes control government through a strict system of distribution based on kinship links and validated by genealogical origins. Genealogical origins provide the ruling tribal factions with the ideological premises on the basis of which the legitimacy of government is sought; they consider their rule to be a given that cannot be challenged by public election or delegation. In Bahrain and Kuwait, where parliamentary elections have been held, members of the ruling families have never run for elected posts on the grounds that what they have earned historically—the right to rule—cannot be forfeited by 'the whims of public opinion'.

Benefits and power in tribally controlled states are distributed on the basis of kinship links; the closer one is to the ruler, the more benefits and power one gets. The pattern is as follows: the ruler's brother becomes prime minister, the ruler's son (the heir apparent) becomes minister of defence, and his cousins and nephews control the other force-oriented ministries and departments: the Ministry of the Interior, the National Guard, immigration and the Air Force. In Saudi Arabia, the seven brothers who were born to Abdulaziz bin Saud of his Sudairi wife (known internally as the Al-Fahd, and externally as 'the Sudairi Seven') continue to occupy the key posts, ministries and departments in the country. Their power is not derived simply from being brothers, but from controlling the decision-making process (Fig. 13). Ministries of a developmental or services nature,

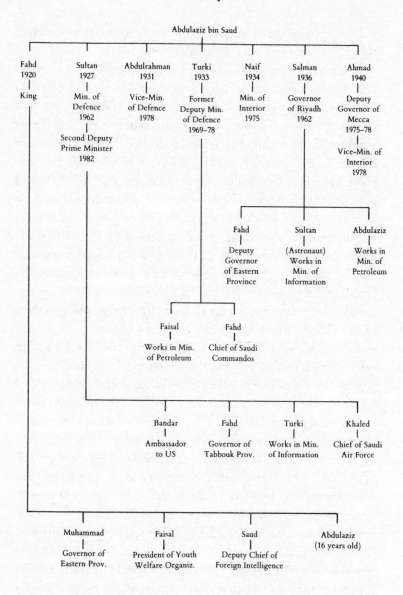

Figure 13: Al-Fahd and the Government Offices they Occupied in Saudi Arabia, 1988

such as Industry, Agriculture, Health and Transport, are allocated to the *madini* faction—the technocrats.

Among the ruling tribal elites, there emerges a kind of orchestra-like arrangement, with each brother handling or relating to a different segment in society. In Bahrain, Isa bin Salman, the ruler, stands for all the citizens; his second brother, Khalifa, who is prime minister, caters for the new, modern, upwardly mobile elites; his youngest brother, Muhammad, handles the religionists; his son, Hamad, the youth clubs. The pattern is repeated in other Gulf countries with some mild modification in kinship links and variations of social groupings. In Saudi Arabia, for example, the sons of Ibn Saud head the power-based ministries and departments, whereas the Al-Shaikh, the descendants of Muhammad Abdulwahhab, the founder of the Wahhabi movement, handle the religiously based ministries such as those of Education and Justice. The Al-Saud and the Al-Shaikh intermarry as a gesture of equality.

In the tribally controlled governments of the Gulf, the ruling tribal elites always seek an alliance with the religionists, the Muslim fundamentalists—this is true of all the Gulf states, including Saudi Arabia. The Arab nationalists constitute the opposition party, not in the Gulf alone but in all Arab countries. Opposition is based on pan-Arabism. The alliance between the ruling tribal elites and the Muslim fundamentalists often adopts the motto, 'The Qur'an is our constitution,' which grants the ruler the freedom to govern without public accountability. This brings to mind a conversation that is supposed to have taken place in the early part of the Umayyad empire. One day a certain Abu Dhur al-Ghafari came to Mu'awiya, the founder of the Umayyad dynasty, and said, 'I protest at your calling the treasury the wealth of God (*mal allah*)!'

'What do you want to call it?'

'I want to call it the wealth of Muslims (*mal al-muslimin*).'

'But why?'

'If you call it *mal allah*, I have no say in how it is spent, but if you call it *mal al-muslimin*, then I do have a say.' 'The-Qur'an-is-our-constitution' policy provides the ruler with the justification for dictating his policy independently of public supervision, thus becoming an autocrat.

And herein lies the key. In Arab states, there is a deliberate policy not to create a public—hence the suppression of free political parties or institutions, which explains the lack of civic life. The question is how to create a public that holds the ruler accountable for his actions and policies. The political agony of Arab countries can be summarized in one sentence: no ruler, whether king, president, prince or sultan, is held accountable for his policies. Only a strong public could make the ruler accountable. Hence, the word '*republic*.' 'The public' has not yet emerged in Arab countries; 'the private' prevails.

It is interesting to note that the word for public in Arabic (*amma*) signifies low achievement. The stress on endogamous behaviour as a desirable model of action makes 'the public' takes on a secondary moral value. What matters is 'the private', the solidarity (*asabiya*) one belongs to; everything else—political rights, civil rights and parliaments—is of questionable value.

Although 'the public' has not emerged yet as a political force, culturally it is being enhanced through an intricate system of convergence which is already taking place throughout the Arab world in speech, dress, food, the arts and worship. Spoken and written Arabic are much closer today than they have ever been. Moreover, there is a clear shift in meaning from religious to nationalistic contexts. For example, *umma*, which was used originally to refer to the Islamic community, is now also used to refer to the Arab nation. Many other concepts, such as *nasr* and *fatih*, have changed meanings in the same way.[1]

Whether or not cultural convergence creates a politically

conscious 'public' depends upon the emergence of political institutions—parliaments, free political parties, a free press, free labour unions, free professional associations, etc—macro-national platforms that cut across endogamous solidarities. Solidarities built upon endogamous practices militate against the rise of a 'public' and subsequently public institutions. This explains why power is seized by solidarities through military coups or countercoups, one-party systems or dynastic rule, but not through popular vote. The parliaments instituted in many Arab states have either been dissolved by political solidarities or have been simply a mirror of autocratic rule. Otherwise it would be difficult to explain how a president receives 99.99% of the vote, a percentage unheard of in any democracy.

The Arabs do not play chess; they play backgammon. They do not rule through the authority of law and office; they dominate autocratically through a fluid chain of *khanats*. It is not surprising that Ayatollah Khumaini of Iran tabooed chess in preference for backgammon, where 'The will of God is more visibly manifested.'

Appendix A
Backgammon

The game starts with player A placing all his stones in *khanat* 1, house 4, which belongs to B; likewise B places his stones in *khanat* 1, house 1 (Fig. 1). With each throw of the dice, while player B moves his stones clockwise from his opponent's house to his own, player A moves in exactly the opposite direction. If the dice show a combination of 4:5 a player can move one or two stones 4 or 5 steps respectively.

Once a player has succeeded in moving all his stones across the board to his house, he starts to 'eat' (remove) them depending on the *khanat* in which they are placed. If the dice show 5:3, the player eats one stone from *khanat* 5 and one from *khanat* 3. If there are no stones in *khanat* 3, the player moves one from a higher *khanat* to a lower one. If no stones are available in higher *khanats*, then the player eats a stone available in the next lowest *khanat*.

Double dice such as 6:6 or 2:2 are played four times six or four times two. The player who finishes eating his 15 stones first wins the game. In *franjiya* and *mahbusa*, 3 games out of 5 and 5 games out of 9 usually win the match respectively.

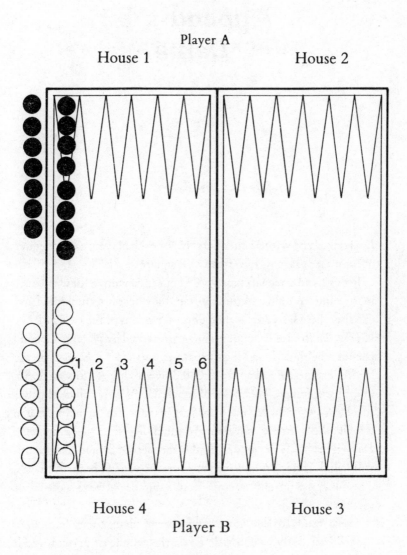

Figure 1: The Backgammon Board

Appendix B
Dama

Dama is played with 32 chequers, 16 for each player; each chequer occupies a square in two rows of 8 squares each.

Rows 1 and 8 are left empty. Chequers can move forward only in the same column and step by step; they become vulnerable and can therefore be 'eaten' when unprotected, as in the case of F4 or F5 (Fig. 2). Isolated chequers can be protected by placing a second chequer behind them, thus creating a group or *khanat*. In the figure, chequer A4 can be protected by moving A2 to square A3; or C5 by moving C7 behind it to square C6. When a black chequer reaches row 8 or a red one row 1, it becomes an imam or *dama* in which case it moves on the board much like the Queen in chess. *Dama* is probably derived from the verbal root *damina* (*dawmana* in colloquial Arabic), which means 'to rest assured or be guaranteed'. The player who gets a *dama* first is almost always assured of victory.

Dama tends to be more widespread than backgammon; a 'board' can easily be constructed on the ground or in sand, and it can be played with 4, 5, 6 or 7 columns and rows. In the Syrian desert around Palmyra I have seen it played on sand with stones and camel droppings.

Player A

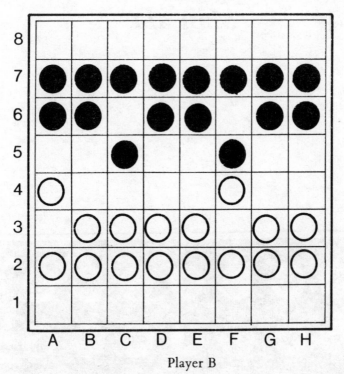

Player B

Figure 2: The *Dama* Board

Appendix C
Man'ala

Player A

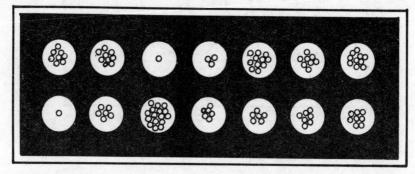

Player B

Figure 3: The *Man'ala* Board

Man'ala (Fig. 3), which is derived from *naqala* (pronounced *na'ala* in the vernacular and meaning to carry from place to place) is a single board with 7 holes each containing 7 pebbles. A player may choose to start from whatever hole he wants: taking all 7 pebbles from this hole, he moves clockwise, dropping 1 pebble in every hole. If the final pebble in his hand falls in an empty hole, his turn ends (vulnerability of isolation). If it falls in a hole containing 2 pebbles (*khanat*) he then 'eats' the 2 plus whatever pebbles happen to be in the opposite hole. In all other situations, he collects all the pebbles in this hole and goes on moving clockwise, dropping 1 pebble in each hole. The players count the pebbles they have 'eaten' and whoever gets to 100 first wins the game.

Appendix D
Beel

Beel is played by children between about 7 and 12, who are beyond infancy and a little before puberty. The players divide into two teams, each selected by a captain, the strong man who gives the team his name. The person who heads the team is never called 'captain' as such; he is referred to by his first name. He plays the role of captain because he selects the team which carries his name, such as Issam's team or Fuad's team. Captains take turns at selecting members of their teams one by one from a 'universe' of potential players available at the time. This selection process involves a great deal of bargaining.

The first bargaining episode centres around who is to start the selection process. If one captain is a better player, he is then pressed to allow the other to start. Or the strong captain might stand alone against two acting as one. If the captains play the game equally well, they flip a coin and the one who guesses correctly starts the selection process. If no coins are available, one of the captains takes a small object such as a pebble or a piece of straw and hides it in his fist. If the other captain correctly identifies the fist in which the object is hidden, he then starts selecting.

As the game does not require a specific number of players—it

can be played with two, three, four, or as many as are available—
the captain who begins the selection process may have the
advantage of an extra player, in which case two players could be
selected to balance a single one. In other words, the captains do
not necessarily choose equal numbers of players, but try to
balance skill against numbers and vice versa. Consequently,
whereas one team may have three players, the other team may
have five or more.

Once the players are divided into two teams, they each proceed
to occupy their territory, called *hima* (the protected land).
Significantly, the same term, *hima*, is used to signify tribal
territories in Arab society. The teams' territories are divided by a
straight line. The game begins with one player from team A
charging against all the players in team B: he crosses the middle
line, roaring rhythmically in a single breath: *beel. . .beel. . .beel.*

If the charging player runs out of breath while still in the
opposing team's territory he is said to be 'dead' and is consequently
eliminated. In fact, members of the opposite team may all gang up
against a charging player and hold him tight until he runs out of
breath while still in their territory. Should this happen, the
charging player is likewise eliminated.

On the other hand, if a player charges against the opposite team
while chanting his *beels*, but manages to touch one of them and get
back to his *hima* without running out of breath, the player he
touches is henceforth eliminated. The game continues with one
player from each team charging against the others until a team
runs out of players, and thus loses. The game continues until one
team wins. There is no time limit; a single match may continue for
one minute or as long as two hours.

While charging against the other team, a player has to be
careful not to be caught out of breath. His team will not come to
his rescue as long as he is in the opposing team's territory. Only
when he manages to get back to his territory will his team rush to

the rescue. However, he can always retreat to his *hima*, where he is safe, to draw breath. If he retreats without touching an opponent he accomplishes nothing. He neither eliminates an opposing player nor is eliminated himself.

The player who charges on his *beels* against the opposite team has to handle all of them simultaneously, one against all. He has to monitor the movements of every single opposing player. He moves slowly but keeps alert, puffing out his *beels* until he spots a player in a weak position, then storms him, touches him and hurriedly races back to his team's territory before he is caught.

In their turn, the opposing team tries to trap the player by fooling him into a seemingly weak position in order to strangle him out of breath. If thus strangled, the player gets nothing more than cheers of encouragement from his team on the other side of the line. If he is physically strong he may pull his stranglers into his team's territory without losing breath; in this case, once he gets one foot inside his own territory, all the stranglers who engaged him are declared 'dead'.

The strongest or fastest are normally chosen to be captains. In order to display their strength or speed, captains are usually the last to charge. The most confident will charge first and finish the match quickly.

Appendix E
Asir

The two teams in *asir* are selected in the same way as in *beel*, but neither occupies a clearly marked territory. The competition centres around the protection of a shrine symbolized by a big stone placed in the middle of an open field. While one team assumes the role of 'defenders' of the shrine, the other team plays the role of 'attackers'. The defenders guard the shrine by trying to prevent any of the attackers laying a foot on the stone. If any of the attackers succeeds in doing so, his team wins the game outright and the first match is over. While putting his foot on the stone, the player cries with a loud voice *sbirrrrrrrrrki*, meaning 'settled down'.

In the meantime, the defenders monitor the movements of all the attackers in the hope of catching them before they lay a foot on the shrine. If an attacker is caught while trying to lay a foot on the stone or trying to cut between the stone and any of the defenders, he is declared 'dead' and is thus eliminated. Once all the attackers are caught, they lose the game. They win only if one of their team lays a foot on the stone or if they succeed in eliminating the defenders one by one by cutting speedily between them and the shrine. While cutting speedily this way, the player cries *qatuuuuu'a*, meaning 'being cut'.

When the first match ends, the teams change roles for the second match, when attackers become defenders and vice versa. The game is played repeatedly until the team tire. They then retire to count their gains and losses. While doing so, reference is always made to the skills displayed by individual players rather than to the general performance of the team as a body. They say, for example, that while Fawwaz was looking westwards, Marwan surprised him from the east and cut him off. Or that Issam, walking slowly on his toes, sneaked up from behind the olive tree, and with the speed of lightning laid his foot on the shrine.

A skilful player must always be on the alert, monitoring the movements of every member of the opposing team, as well as keeping a watchful eye on his own. In order to develop a successful strategy, he has to be constantly ready to map the moving positions of all the players at once, irrespective of whether they belong to his or to the opposing team.

Appendix F
Basra

Like many card games, *basra* can be played with two, three or four players. If with four, two players normally team up against the other two. But in order to increase the element of competition, people often play as individuals, without teams.

In *basra*, or *ashush*, cards are distributed to every player in one lump, in sets of four or six cards at a time. Four other cards are laid face upwards on the floor. The first player, that is the one sitting on the right of the dealer, tries to match the cards on the floor with the cards in his hand: ace matches ace, nine matches nine, king matches king, and so on. The card in the hand 'eats' the card it matches on the floor. If no cards match, the player then has to throw another card on the floor and the next player takes over. The right to deal rotates at every shuffle.

A card in the hand could match the sum of the cards on the floor. For example, 9 matches 6 and 3, 2 and 7, 1 and 8 and 5 and 4. The knave (jack), which is called *ashush*, matches everything; it is an imam that 'eats' everything else on the floor, which is exactly what the term means in colloquial Arabic. In Bahrain, I have heard people referring to the knave as imam.

If a card is laid or left alone on the floor, it becomes vulnerable and could be taken as *basra* should it match a card in the hand. This could happen by manipulating the jack that eats everything else, thus forcing the next player to throw a lone card on the floor (vulnerability of isolation).

The *basra* counts as 10, the ace 1, the knave 1; the ten of diamonds counts as 3, the two of clubs counts as 2, and the player who gets the most cards wins 3 points. The game is won once a player accumulates the sum of 101 points. Aside from the specific cards mentioned above, other cards carry equivalent values with no distinction made between diamonds or hearts, clubs or spades, kings or queens, sevens or fours. The highest value obviously is placed upon the *basra*, which is a captured lone card, or a 'hostage'.

Notes

Chapter 1

1. This is an Ibadi saying.

2. These games include *asir, mistkhibayi, sakkif sakkif al-irmi, hmara tawila, dabahna al-anza, laqut, qamu, dawsh, di'kira.*

3. In the present book, the number of the *sura* precedes the number of the verse. For example, 3/103 means *sura* 3, verse 103.

Chapter 2

1. Versions of this chapter have appeared in *International Journal of Sociology of the Family*, vol. II, no. 2 (July-Dec. 1981) and in Wadad al-Qadi (ed.), *Studia Arabica and Islamica*, American University of Beirut Press, Beirut, 1981.

2. The legal aspect has been intensively studied by Islamic jurists who deliberate on property, inheritance, debt, marriage, divorce, authority and succession. The behavioural aspect deals with standardized and patterned actions associated with particular family relationships. The corporational approach, which is characteristic of anthropological studies, deals with the mechanisms of group formation, the collective action of kinship groups, and the principles of group alignment, recruitment and opposition. The linguistic model, on the other hand, uses kinship terms for the purpose of cognitive mapping or componential analysis; this is to discover the underlying psycho-cultural themes through cross-cultural comparisons. To my knowledge, this approach has not yet been used in the study of Arab kinship systems.

3. See, for example, Peters (1963) for peasants; Khuri (1975: 21–30) for suburbs; Bujra (1971) for towns; and Musil (1928) for nomads.

4. See Ibn Manzur (1955: 301–7) for more details.

5. See Antoun (1968b) on family names as a system of social control.

6. This has an interesting effect on the proliferation of segments of kinship groups.

7. The letter 'i' at the end of the word signifies 'my'.

Chapter 3

1. These motives were each considered at length in Khuri (1970).

2. This is based on a house-to-house survey carried out in the Beirut suburbs of Chiyah and Ghobeire between 1967 and 1969.

3. It should be noted here that the practice of clitoridectomy, which is prevalent among the Coptic peasants of Upper Egypt and the Muslim Nubians of the Sudan, and the widespread practice among the Arabs of dyeing parts of the head, hands and feet with *henna*, are both specifically intended to control girls' emotions.

4. See Table 3 for abbreviations.

Chapter 4

1. A more theoretical version of this chapter was published in Khuri (1968).

2. This statement is made in reference to Khadduri's (1952: 37–8) work in which he views bargaining as the shopkeeper's job performed for fun, a game, he says, often interrupted by irrelevant topics of conversation; and also to Hamady (1960: 37), who uses bargaining to illustrate 'the subjective, personal dealings of the Arab'—this is where, according to Hamady, the Arab combines social duty, business and pleasure.

Chapter 5

1. A version of this chapter appeared in Khuri (1976).

2. The data were collected between January 1967 and December 1969. The figure of 575 households is taken from al-Aswad (1910: 592). Al-Aswad was the secretary of the tax-collecting office in Ba'abda town (Mount Lebanon), about 16 km from Chiyah. The other figures, 5,000 households and 30,000 people, are taken from the census carried out during my research project between 1967 and 1969.

3. The Husainis from Byblos; the Musawis from Nabi Shit; the Murtadas from Baalbek; the al-Amins from the village of Shaqra in the district of Nabatiya; and the Sharaf al-Dins, the Safyi al-Dins and the Subhs, all from Tyre.

Chapter 6

1. *Ashab nufudh* (possessors of influence), *ashab sha'biya* (possessors of popularity), *ahl alaqat* (men of contacts), *buyut ma'rufa* (prominent 'houses'), *sudur* (fronts), *a'yan* (eyes), *wujaha* (faces) and *ru'asa* (heads) of the community.

2. Salman Rushdie, *The Satanic Verses*, Viking, London, 1988.

Chapter 7

1. For details see Khuri (1990: 218).

Glossary

WORD IN TEXT	PRONOUNCIATION	MEANING
ab(i)	*'ab ('abī)*	father (my father)
abna(i)	*'abnā' ('abnā'ī)*	sons (my sons)
adala	*'adala*	to balance
adil	*'adīl*	wife's sister's husband
afandi	*'afandī*	notable (status title)
afta	*'aftā*	to resolve
agha	*'āghā*	notable (status title)
ahala	*'ahala*	to rehabilitate
ahfad	*'ahfād*	predecessors
ahl	*'ahl*	parents; family
ahl-dhumma	*'ahl-dhumma*	the protected
ahl-mantiq	*'ahl-manṭiq*	possessors of eloquence
a'ila (a'ilat)	*'ā'ila*	family; children
a'iliya	*'ā'ilīya*	familial
akh(i)	*'akh ('akhī)*	brother (my brother)
akhawat		sisters; collective
[pl. of *ukht*]	*'akhawāt*	solidarity
akhawiya	*'akhawīya*	brotherly
akhdar	*'akhḍar*	green
akhira (al-)	*'ākhira*	the other world (after death)
ala	*'āla*	to provide

151

ala	'ala	to be elevated
allah	'allāh	God
alim	'ālim	scientist; knowing the future
amal	'amal	work
amara	'amara	to order; instruct
amara	'amāra	section of tribe; building
amir	'amīr	tribal chief
amm	'amm	father's brother
amma	'amma	father's sister
amma	'āmma	the commoners; the public
ammara	'ammara	to build
ansab	'ansāb	traceable genealogies
ansar	'anṣār	partisans
ariba	'ariba	to increase
arrab	'arrāb	godfather
arraba	'arrāba	godmother
asabiya	'aṣabīya	solidarity
asara	'asara	to capture
asbat [pl. of sibt]	'asbāt	predecessors; linkages
ashab asl [pl. of sahib]	'aṣḥāb 'aṣl	possessors of origin
ashara	'āshara	to seduce; tease; befriend
ashira	'ashīra	clan
ashush	'āīshūsh	a card game
asil	'aṣīl	in-bred
asir	'asīr	captive
asl	'aṣl	origin
asliyun (al-)	'aṣlīyūn	original
asyad [pl. of sayyid]	'asyād	master; descendant of imam
awlad [pl. of walad]	'awlād	boys; sons; children

awqaf	'awqāf	religious endowment
azl (al-)	'azl	isolation
badil	badīl	equivalent
bait	bait	household; home; family
ba'l	ba'l	husband
bani-khudair	banī-khudair	sons of green
basra	bāsra	a card game
bata	bāta	to spend the night; stay
batn	baṭn	1. belly 2. section of a tribe
beel	bīl	a game
bey	bey	notable (status title)
bila asl	bilā 'aṣl	lacking origin
bint	bint	daughter
bi'sa	bi'sa	[how] miserable
dala	dāla	to rotate power
dama	ḍāma	a game
damina	ḍamina	assured; guaranteed
dawla	dawla	state; title of prime minister
dawmana	ḍawmana	assured; guaranteed
dhu hadrat	dhū ḥaḍrat	possessor of presence
din (al-)	dīn	religion
dunya (al-)	dunyā	this world
emir	emīr	prince
fadila	faḍīla	Muslim religious shaikh
fadula	faḍula	to be virtuous
fakhama	fakhāma	great; title of presidents
fakhidh	fakhidh	1. thigh 2. section of a tribe
fakhuma	fakhuma	to become great
faqih	faqīh	Islamic jurist

fasala	*faṣala*	to separate
fasila	*faṣīla*	1. species 2. section of a tribe
fatih (al-)	*fatiḥ*	conquest
firash (li-l-)	*firāsh*	bed
franjiya	*franjīya*	Western
ghibta	*ghibṭa*	1. happiness 2. Christian patriarch
ghitra	*ghiṭra*	headcloth
ghuraba (al-)	*ghurabā'*	foreigners
habl	*ḥabl*	rope or cable
hadith	*ḥadīth*	Islamic traditions
hakawati	*ḥakawātī*	narrator
hama	*ḥama*	1. to protect 2. mother-in-law
hamada	*ḥamada*	to thank
hamdu		
li-allah (al-)	*al-ḥamdu li-'allāh*	thanks be to God
hamu	*ḥamū*	father-in-law
harama	*ḥarama*	to forbid
harbou	*ḥarboū'*	tactician
hasab	*ḥasab*	matrilineal male predecessors
hashr (al-)	*ḥashr*	crowding
hima	*ḥimā*	tribal land
hurma	*ḥurmā*	1. taboo 2. wife 3. woman
ibn	*'ibn*	son
ibna	*'ibna*	daughter
ightabata	*'ightabaṭa*	to be happy
ijtahada	*'ijtahada*	to interpret
ikhwa(-n)	*'ikhwa*	
[pl. of *akh*]	(*'ikhwān*)	brothers; collective solidarity
ilm	*'ilm*	science; knowledge

imam	*'imām*	leader in prayer; top Shi'a official; divine designation
imra'a	*'imra'a*	wife; woman
in sha'a allah	*'in shā'a 'allāh*	if God so wishes
iqal	*'iqāl*	rope-like ribbon for headdress
ird (al-)	*'irḍ*	honour
ishbin	*'ishbīn*	best man
ishbina	*'ishbīna*	female equivalent of *ishbin*
islamiya (al-)	*'islāmīya*	Islamic
iyal	*'īyāl*	children
jabba	*jabba*	to cut; fertilize
jadd	*jadd*	grandfather
jadda	*jadda*	grandmother
jalala	*jalāla*	title of kings
jalla	*jalla*	to rise high
janab hadirtak	*janāb ḥaḍirtak*	Your Lordship
jizya	*jizya*	punishment; tax
jubb	*jubb*	1. tribal division; cluster 2. well
jumhur	*jumhūr*	tribal division; crowd
kanna	*kanna*	to stay quietly
khal	*khāl*	maternal uncle
khala	*khāla*	maternal aunt
khalaf (al-)	*khalaf*	successors
khalafa	*khalafa*	to succeed; conspire
khalida (al-)	*khālida*	eternal
khanat(s)	*khānat*	entry; equal(s); social solidarity
khassa	*khāṣṣa*	the private ones
khataba	*khaṭaba*	to lecture
khatib	*khaṭīb*	public speaker; imam

khwaiyan	*khwaīyān*	diminutive form of *akh* (brother)
kinna (kinni)	*kinna (kinnī)*	daughter-in-law
kufiya	*kūfīya*	headcloth
la ansab	*lā 'ansāb*	no traceable genealogies
ma sha'a allah	*mā shā'a 'allāh*	whatever God wishes
ma'ali	*ma'ālī*	title of minister
madani	*madanī*	urban
ma'dhun	*ma'dhūn*	Islamic jurist
maghrabiya	*maghrabīya*	from al-Maghrib (Morocco)
mahbusa	*maḥbūsa*	captivity
mal	*māl*	wealth
malaki (al-)	*malakī*	kingly
man'ala	*man'ala*	a game
maru'a	*maru'a*	to become dignified
ma'ruf	*ma'rūf*	known; prominent
mashlah	*mashlaḥ*	robe
masturun	*mastūrūn*	self-sufficient
maysurun	*maysūrūn*	affluent
mir'iz	*mir'iz*	a rare species of goat
mufti	*muftī*	Islamic jurist
muhtajun	*muḥtājūn*	poor; needy
mujtahid	*mujtahid*	Shi'a jurist
mulk	*mulk*	possession; wealth
mulla	*mulla*	Shi'a specialist
mu'minun (al-)	*mu'minūn*	faithful
muslimin (al-)	*muslimīn*	the Muslims
mustad'afun (al-)	*mustaḍ'afūn*	the made weak
muwali	*muwālī*	affiliated

nafa	*nafā*	to overlook
nafs al-a'ila	*nafs al-'ā'ila*	the same family
nafs al-shai	*nafs al-shaī'*	the same thing
najis	*najis*	spiritually polluted
naqala	*naqala; na'ala*	to move places
nasab	*nasab*	patrilineality; alliance
nasaba	*nasaba*	to trace genealogically
nasib	*naṣīb*	husband
nasiba	*naṣība*	wife
nasr (al-)	*naṣr*	victory
na'zum	*na'zum*	we intend
ni'ma	*ni'ma*	[how] graceful
niyafa	*nīyāfa*	title of Christian bishop
pasha	*bāshā*	notable (status title)
qabala	*qabala*	to seek direction
qabali	*qabalī*	tribal
qabila (qabili)	*qabīla (qabīlī)*	tribe
qadi	*qāḍī*	judge
qa'id	*qā'id*	leader
qala	*qāla*	to say
qarib	*qarīb*	close
qaruba	*qaruba*	to be close
qataba	*qaṭaba*	to collect
qatriba	*qaṭrība*	wife's daughter
qatu'a	*qāṭū'a*	being cut
qurba	*qurba*	relatives; neighbours
qutb	*quṭb*	leader
raba	*raba*	to increase
rabiba	*rabība*	father's wife

raht	*raḥṭ*	1. tribal division
		2. active crowd
ra'is	*ra'īs*	head; president
ra'isa	*ra'isa*	to head
rajila	*rajila*	to walk
rajul	*rajul*	1. leg 2. husband
risala (al-)	*risāla*	message
sabbaha	*sabbaḥa*	to praise
sada	*sāda*	to prevail
sadaqa	*ṣadaqa*	alms
sahaba (al-)	*ṣaḥāba*	companions of the Prophet
sahara	*ṣahara*	to weld
sahib	*ṣāḥib*	friend; the possessor of
sahib al-sumuw	*ṣāḥib al-sumuw*	
al-malaki	*al-malakī*	Lord Royal Highness
sahib asl	*ṣāḥib 'aṣl*	possessing origin
salaf (al-)	*salaf*	predecessors
salafa	*salafa*	to make [soil] even
samaha	*samāḥa*	title of imam or mufti
samuha	*samuḥa*	to be forgiving or generous
satr	*satr*	to cover; protect
sayyid	*sayyid*	master; descendant of imam
sha'a	*shā'a*	to wish
sha'aba	*sha'aba*	to drift
sha'b	*sha'b*	people; nation
shabab (al-)	*shabāb*	youth
shaikh	*shaikh*	chief; Islamic jurist
shakha	*shākha*	to become old
shari'a	*sharī'a*	Islamic law
shirha	*shirḥa*	appeal for financial aid
shura (al-)	*shūra*	sounding out individual
		opinion

sibt (al-)	sibṭ	from the Prophet's predecessors
sibt (al-) la'in (al-)	sibṭ la'īn	the accursed *sibt*
sibt al-rasul	sibṭ al-rasūl	the Prophet's daughter's sons
sidi	sīdī	lord or master
sihr	ṣihr	1. son-in-law 2. sister's husband
silf	silf	husband's brother
silfa	silfa	husband's brother's wife
silsila	silsila	chain
siyada (al-)	sīyāda	sovereignty
sukkan (al-)	sukkān	inhabitants
sulala	sulāla	genealogy
su'luq	ṣu'lūq	small
sumuw (al-)	sumuw	title for Prince Highness
suq	sūq	market
ta'adud	ta'āḍuḍ	pillar to pillar
tabaqa	ṭabaqa	social class
tabriya	tabrīya	becoming innocent
tahaluf	taḥāluf	alliance
taiyar	ṭaīyār	pilot; free
takatuf	takātuf	shoulder to shoulder
tal	ṭāl	prolonged
tal umrak	ṭāl 'umrak	may your life be prolonged
tasalsul	tasalsul	descent
ta'sil	ta'ṣīl	in-breeding
tawil	ṭawīl	long
ukht(i)	'ukht ('ukhtī)	sister (my sister)
ukhuwwa (al-)	'ukhuwwa	brotherhood
ulama	'ulamā'	Islamic religious men

umm	*'umm*	mother
umma (al-)	*'umma*	community
umr (al-)	*'umr*	life
umrak	*'umrak*	your life
umran	*'umrān*	civilization
umumi	*'umūmī*	public
usra	*'usra*	nuclear family
usul	*'uṣūl*	[those who are] in-bred
wajh	*wajh*	face
walad (al-)	*walad*	boy; son
warathat	*warathat*	heirs
ya tawil al-umr	*yā ṭawīl al-'umr*	ye. . .of long life
yahzumun	*yaḥzumūn*	they enact
yalla	*yalla*	carry on (colloquial)
yawm al-hashr	*yawm al-ḥashr*	day of judgement
yu'assil	*yu'aṣṣil*	to in-breed
za'ama	*za'ama*	to assume
za'im	*za'īm*	status title; national leader
zakat	*zakāt*	tax; form of sacrifice
zawj	*zawj*	husband
zawja	*zawja*	wife
zawwaja	*zawwaja*	to pair
zu'ama	*zu'amā'*	pl. of *za'im*

Bibliography

Abu-Lughod, Janet (1971) *Cairo*. Princeton: Princeton University Press.

Ali, Jawad (1976) *Tarikh al-Arab qabl al-Islam* (History of the Arabs before Islam). Beirut: Dar al-Ilm li-l-Malayin. (In Arabic).

Ammar, Hamed (1954) *Growing up in an Egyptian Village*. London: Routledge & Kegan Paul.

Antoun, Richard (1968a) 'On the Modesty of Women in Arab Muslim Villages: a Study in the Accommodation of Traditions', *American Anthropologist* 70:671–97.

_____ (1968b) 'On the Significance of Names in an Arab Village', *Ethnology* 8:158–70.

_____ (1972) *Arab Village*. Bloomington: Indiana University Press.

al-Aswad, Ibrahim (1910) *Dalil Lubnan* (A Guide to Lebanon). Beirut: Catholic University Press. (In Arabic).

Barclay, Harold (1964) *Buurri al-Lamaab*. Ithaca: Cornell University Press.

Bujra, A.S. 1971. *The Politics of Stratification*. Oxford: Clarendon Press.

Burgess, Ernest W. (1938) 'Residential Segregation', in Miller Alihan (ed.), *Social Ecology*. New York: Columbia University Press.

Cohen, Abner (1965) *Arab Border Villages in Israel: A Study of Continuity and Change in Social Organization*. Manchester: Manchester University Press.

Eickelman, Dale (1976) *Moroccan Islam*. Austin: University of Texas Press.

Geertz, Clifford (1968) *Islam Observed*. New Haven: Yale University Press.

Gellner, Ernest (1981) *Muslim Society*. Cambridge: Cambridge University Press.

Granqvist, Hilma (1931) *Marriage Conditions in a Palestinian Village* (Commentat. hum. Litt. 3:8). Helsinki: Societas Scientiarum Fennica.

—————— (1935) *Marriage Conditions in a Palestinian Village* (Commentat. hum. Litt. 6:8). Helsinki: Societas Scientiarum Fennica.

Gulick, John (1955) *Social Structure and Culture Change in a Lebanese Village*. New York: Werner Gren Foundation.

—————— (1969) 'Village and City: Cultural Continuities in Twentieth-Century Middle Eastern Cultures', in Ira M. Lapidus (ed.), *Middle Eastern Cities*. Berkeley: University of California Press.

—————— (1976) *The Middle East: An Anthropological Perspective*. Pacific Palisades, Calif: Goodyear Publishing Co.

Hamady, Sania (1960) *Temperament and Character of the Arabs*. New York: Twayne Publishers.

Hatab, Zuhayr (1976) *Tatwir Buna al-Usra al-Arabiya* (Evolution of Arab Family Structure). Beirut: Arab Development Institute. (In Arabic).

Homans, G. C. (1951) *The Human Group*. London: Routledge & Kegan Paul.

Ibn Manzur (1955) *Lisan al-Arab* (The Tongue of the Arabs). Beirut: Dar Sadir. (In Arabic).

Kashifulghata, Muhammad al-Husain (n.d.) *Asl al-Shi'a wa Usuluha* (Shi'a Origin and Principles). Beirut: Maktabat al-Urfan. (In Arabic).

Khadduri, Majid (1952) 'Governments of the Arab East', *Journal of International Affairs* 6:37–48.

Khumaini, Ayatollah (1979) *al-Hukuma al-Islamiya* (The Islamic Republic). Beirut: Dar al-Tali'a. (In Arabic).

Khuri, Fuad I. (1968) 'The Etiquette of Bargaining in the Middle East', *American Anthropologist* 70:698–706.

_____ (1970) 'Parallel Cousin Marriage Reconsidered', *Man* 5:597–618.

_____ (1975) *From Village to Suburb*. Chicago: University of Chicago Press.

_____ (1976) 'A Profile of Family Associations in Two Suburbs of Beirut', in J.G. Peristiany (ed.), *Mediterranean Family Structures*. Cambridge: Cambridge University Press, pp. 81–100.

_____ (1987) 'The Ulama: A Comparative Study of Sunni and Shi'a Religious Officials', *Middle Eastern Studies* 23:291–312.

_____ (1988) *Imamat al-Shahid wa Imamat al-Batal* (The Organization of Religion among Islamic Sects). Beirut: University Publishing House. (In Arabic).

_____ (1990) *Imams and Emirs*. London: Saqi Books.

Mas'ud, J. (1964) *al-Ra'id* [the leading dictionary]. Beirut: Dar al-Ilm lil-Malayin. (In Arabic).

Musil, Alois (1928) *The Manners and Customs of Rwala Bedouins*. New York: American Geographical Society.

Peters, Emrys (1960) 'The Proliferation of Segments in the Lineage of the Bedouin in Cyrenaica', *Journal of the Royal Anthropological Institute of Great Britain and Ireland* 90:29–53.

_____ (1963) 'Aspects of Rank and Status among Muslims in a Lebanese Village', in J. Pitt-Rivers (ed.), *Mediterranean Countrymen*. Paris: Mouton, pp. 159–202.

_____ (1967) 'Some Structural Aspects of the Feud among the Camel-Herding Bedouin of Cyrenaica', *Africa* 37:261–82.

_____ (1976) 'Aspects of Affinity in a Lebanese Maronite Village', in J.G. Peristiany (ed.), *Mediterranean Family Structures*. Cambridge: Cambridge University Press, pp. 27–79.

Prothro, Terry and Lutfi Diab (1974) *Changing Family Patterns in the Arab East*. Beirut: American University of Beirut Press.

Rosenfeld, Henry (1958) 'Process of Structural Change within the Arab Village Extended Family', *American Anthropologist* 60:1127–39.

———— (1968) 'Change, Barriers to Change, and Contradictions in the Arab Village Family', *American Anthropologist* 70:732–51.

Wolf, Arthur (1968) 'Adopt a Daughter-in-law, Marry a Sister: a Chinese Solution to the Problem of the Incest Taboo', *American Anthropologist* 70:864–74.

Index